CW00557962

Working Times

To
Brigid Callaghan

Working Times

Libby Purves

Robinson Publishing
London

First published 1993 by
Robinson Publishing
7 Kensington Church Court
London W8 4SP

Copyright © Libby Purves 1993
Illustrations © Frank Dickens 1993

The last verse of Philip Larkin's poem 'Toads Revisited'
on page 5 is from *Whitsun Weddings*, published
by Faber and Faber 1964 and quoted by kind permission

The right of Libby Purves to be identified as author of
this work, has been asserted by her in accordance with the
Copyright, Designs and Patents Act, 1988

All rights reserved. No part of this publication may be
reproduced in any form or by any means without the prior
written permission of Robinson Publishing

A cataloguing in publication record for this book is
available from the British Library

ISBN 1 85487 237 0

Typeset by Hewer Text Composition Services, Edinburgh
Printed and bound in Great Britain by
Mackays of Chatham PLC, Chatham, Kent

Contents

Acknowledgements

Most of these pieces appeared first, in a shorter form, in *The Times* during 1992. Obvious thanks are due to the paper's then editor, Simon Jenkins, for giving them houseroom. Particular gratitude is owed also to the Features Editor and all her staff (and indeed to numbers of friends and relations in other trades) for feeding me forcibly down the telephone with themes concerning the workplace, and grudges which Ought to be Aired, preferably in a heavily disguised form. After a few weeks, this game was joined with enthusiasm by readers, to whom I also give thanks: I have learned more unprintable things about other people's jobs than I ever thought to, and there was never the slightest risk of running out of subjects. If there had been, I could always have turned yet again to my inexhaustible pool of brothers, Michael, Patrick and Andrew, who have had so many jobs between them (from official Milk Marketing Board parachuting gorilla to folksinging solicitor to brewery barrel-roller and freelance car jockey) that they further extend my vicarious experience.

I suppose I also ought to thank all those other people who have ever employed me, from Mrs Scott at the ice-cream shop in 1961 to the long, and longsuffering, series of producers of Midweek on Radio 4. I would like them all to know that I have been, believe it or not, grateful.

Introduction

I had a very hip, New Age GP once who harangued me on the proper way for a woman in late pregnancy to carry on. 'Try,' he said, 'to think peaceful, happy thoughts. Listen to music and walk through the autumn leaves. The baby will feel it with you.'

Clutching shiftily at my briefcase, I tried to tell him that personally I got my most peaceful happy thoughts when I had just cornered a good story, done the piece or the tape against time, and seen it published or broadcast ahead of the pack. 'Wouldn't the baby enjoy that too?' I asked hopefully. 'I'm sure a foetus would love the happy thoughts you get when you really screw the opposition and then go down to the pub.' He couldn't see it. Autumn leaves were firmly prescribed, and the strange empty stillness of a daytime house. The baby shared the boredom, and on emerging weeks later was manically busy, eyes swivelling around for something to do, mobiles to swipe or milk to suck. Action and achievement were programmed into him.

There is nothing intrinsically wrong with home life. Or leaves. It was just that in his estimate of life's pleasures the doctor discounted one of the greatest. Work. More specifically, going to work. Man the hunter has always known the elation of leaving the cave in the morning to join his hunting-pack (or factory, office, shop, common-room). Never mind the boredom and hardship and exploitation, admit it: there is pleasure in going to work.

And not just the pleasure of achieving the job you came to do. Nobody has ever written a bestseller on The Joy of Colleagues, but

1

there is such a joy. Why not? After all, comradeship is an easier thing, a looser garment, than anyone's family or love-life. It can be satisfying and even restful to spend the day conducting human encounters on the mere basis of logic, reasonable good nature and commercial honour, without people bursting into tears and accusing you of not loving them. Even if they do, you can glance at your watch and invoke the higher good: say, morning conference. Or a train to Cardiff.

Office jokes flourish, the best of them as black and bitter as truffles, cropping up at times of crisis. In early 1992 when I first began writing Working Life for *The Times* newspaper, the best office jokes were occurring inside Maxwell-hit companies ('they found the body, circling some sharks'). The jokes told in offices have the added frisson of exclusivity, and rarely transplant to the outer world without disaster: Gerald Ratner's gag about the earrings which cost the same as a prawn sandwich 'only the sandwich lasts longer' had been circulating around his companies for years before he incautiously let it out at a pompous conference and dished his business. And there are tribal anecdotes in the police force which even long-serving police wives find pretty hard to swallow. I once spent a convivial dinner sitting between a police surgeon and a deputy chief constable, and occasionally they would forget I was there and start reminiscing. 'They never did find the other head, did you know George – ' one would begin, and go on from there.

In this century women have got their feet well under the office table, and we have discovered that we like it too. When mistresses and maids alike flooded into the factories and offices in the First World War they discovered the burden of dual responsibilities, but also the relief of allowing the tangled, tender, painful skein of family life to be spun for a while into the straightforward, cheerful thread of working in a team. It did not matter whether they were working as a Lady Typewriter or a tram conductress, because each of them had – in addition to long hours and fatigue – the chance to tune into that buzz and hum of communal working life. Their rural ancestresses, of course, had known this too, working alongside men in the fields as well as in sewing circles, dairies and other 'women's work'. If you want a celebration of the mutual support of colleaguehood, go no further than the chapters of *Tess of the d'Urbervilles* where she, and Angel, and the other girls work in Talbothays dairy together. It

2

was only the brief historical interlude of urbanization and clear separation of tasks which cut so many women off, for so much of their lives, from the pleasures of teamwork. And, occasionally, of running the joint.

It is a modern truism that – because of the increasing participation of women, and because of men's increasing desire to take some part in family life other than handing over the housekeeping money – our working structures should become more flexible and demand less than total absorption from their employees. I would not argue with that. I have (and my family has) benefited from one of the few truly flexible professions around. But when *The Times* asked me, for a period, to attempt a column called Working Life, I found that I was increasingly inclined to celebrate the status quo – with all its illogicalities, unfairnesses and minor lunacies. The odd squib of dissent had to be thrown in, but all in all I realized almost to my surprise that working life is, prevailingly, OK. A life-enhancer: and not only for those in allegedly glamorous jobs.

For instance, a lot of guff is talked about modems and faxes and how the future lies in telecommuting from the spare bedroom. Myself, I have been doing just this for ten years and am less convinced. Useful as it can be, remote-control teamwork has its drawbacks. People working alone get depressed and lonely: the cat sneers, small snubs rankle, you starve for gossip and the company of peers. After all, even reps on the road develop cosy trade-fair friendships, and nannies gang up thankfully with other nannies in the park. And the commuters on an early Monday morning may look gloomy, but most of them would look gloomier still if the train turned back and delivered them into the muck and muddle of home. After the lonely flat and the complicated love-life, the claustrophobia of babycare or the suburban sameness of a yellowing marriage, it is good to plug into the wider world.

And into wider friendships. Few of us lack at least one ally when the boss is vile, the management batty, the pension scheme nicked and half your desk reallocated to some pushy little jerk. Sometimes those working alliances grow larger than the ones outside. Sometimes they spill out disastrously. But, on balance, they are worth it. All of us – bar a few solitary artists – need the company of colleagues and the sense of being a team player. One of the tragedies of high modern unemployment is that so many people

3

are savagely cut off from this: it is hard to decide whether it is worse for the sixteen-year-old who never had a chance, or the fifty-year-old cut off in his prime with little hope of getting back.

These pieces, collected here and mainly from *The Times*, explore aspects of work and working moods. They are not necessarily about what I do myself. Being incurably nosy, and the recipient of many highly entertaining letters, I have come to discover all sorts of feelings which turn out to lie equally beneath the surface of such different pools as banking, medicine and managing sports centres. Nonetheless, I ought to play fair and offer a brief account of where I start from.

Before I married, I was very much a team player. All doubts, uncertainties and identity crises were soothed and resolved at work. Through the night shift operating BBC control desks at Bush House, working seven days a week on a local radio station, or forming part of the eccentric society of Radio 4 Today producers and reporters, I happily lost myself in teams and tribes. The experience was heightened by odd hours: insane twenty-two-hour shifts lasting from noon until 10 am the next day may be bad for private life, but they do wonders for the intuitive, comradely, slightly hysterical type of office bonding which during those years characterized the Today programme.

All this ended when I became a working mother. For ten years I virtuously eschewed all inessential professional events: six o'clock drinks, long lunches and office parties. I ran home to my children and I do not for a moment regret it. But after that decade a crisis overcame me, and I suddenly found myself meeting an ordinary professional setback with such defeatism, such violent depths of sadness and alienation and confusion, that it briefly rocked my life. And I found to my surprise (and humiliation) that I could not write or think about writing any longer, and that neither husband nor children nor school-gate neighbours were any help at all. Possessor of an apparently happy, balanced existence, I had allowed one element to go missing. I suddenly craved workmates. I needed to talk to people who did what I do, who knew the particular highs and lows of my particular job, and who would accept me as part of their tribe.

Happily, I found the support I had apparently been starving for. Through a number of rather drunken meals and sessions of leaning on office radiators and reminiscing with old cronies, my confidence slowly returned. But it taught me a lesson. Never be thrown off-track by all this New Age, New Man, Me-generation stuff about 'getting in touch with yourself', 'nurturing the inner child' and considering the personal as far more important than the corporate life. Have a home life by all means, but don't throw out the baby with the bathwater. Nourish the inner office-worker for a change.

Because work counts. It is another vital bridge to the rest of the human race – at least as vital as family and marriage, and in these parlous days often longer-lasting. It is up to us to make working environments which are a force for good, which regenerate and nourish our souls as well as our wallets. We need this. Philip Larkin caught the atmosphere in his poem about the 'toad work':

> When the lights come on at four
> At the end of another year?
> Give me your arm, old Toad;
> Help me down Cemetery Road.

1

Off home early, then?

*M*y first job was in a British merchant bank in Hamburg. I typed Bills of Lading in German: sometimes to this day my fingers take on a life of their own and flicker out at lightning speed the words *& Cie.GmbH* or *Aktiengesellschaft* in the middle of a harmless article. Meanwhile I find my back straightening and my feet clicking together under the table, as if I were once more under the eye of Frau Seier and Frau Haas. They ran a tight ship, those ladies: it was understood that one arrived at five to nine – not 9 o'clock; one went out for lunch sharp at one, whether one felt like it or not; wiping the sauerkraut from one's lips one returned at 1.45 and remained static until five. One did not go swanning off to lean on the photocopier, or spend more than three minutes in the Ladies: one worked. If there were no Bills of Lading one sat demurely waiting for more, or took instruction in the German language from Frau Seier. She liked to give me a proverb a day to memorize: *Ohne Fleis, kein Preis* (without labour is no reward) was a favourite of hers. So was *Morgen, Morgen, nur nicht heute sagen aller faulen Leute* which translates as 'Tomorrow, tomorrow, not today, is what the lazy people say!' You will understand my awed nostalgia for these days when I tell you that Frau S. was only twenty, two years older than me. And this was in 1968, when the London office scene meant feckless dollybirds with hangovers: when I stayed with a schoolfriend who was temping in Shepherd Market, I nearly fainted with shock at the reckless informality of her office. Since then I have never made the mistake of thinking that the Germans got richer than us by accident.

But the great thing about that office was that when 5 o'clock came, it emptied. All the men, who had removed their jackets to reveal a dismal vista of string vests worn under transparent white nylon shirts, put them back on and vamoosed. Us girls switched out the desk lamps and followed, exchanging the odd proverb ('All that glisters is not gold, Fraulein Purves! Guten nacht!' 'Schön danke, Frau Seier! Without labour is no reward!') Idyllic, really.

Because at least one knew where one stood. One had served one's hours. Since then my destiny, like that of countless others, has lain in more unstructured workplaces. People drift in between nine and whenever, eat sandwiches while on the phone one day and vanish to John Lewis's for three hours the next; they are still riffling through filing-cabinets when the cleaners turn up at six. Some have keys, and go out to the pub for two hours before returning to 'clear up a few little jobs' at their desk and spill a can of diet soda into the word-processor. The next morning someone else will beat the rush hour by turning up at 7.30, and will absentmindedly swig the flat dregs of the Diet Coke before discovering there is a fag-end in it. Someone else is working from home, or engaged in some baroque jobshare which involves either both parties turning up and getting in one another's way, or else vanishing in a joint flurry of faxes. Increasingly in all fields, one rings people in their offices to be told, 'I'm not sure whether she's due in this morning' or 'Probably about eleven, he's been on a course.' Frau Seier wouldn't like it one bit. Ordnung muss sein. *GmbH. Aktiengesellschaft.* Sorry.

I actually rather approve of flexible hours, being a disciple of the business guru Charles Handy who says that it is degrading to buy people's time rather than their achievement. But human nature tends towards one-upmanship, and flexible working is a perfect lever for making one's fellow-man uncomfortable. Plant a bugged briefcase in any workplace and before long you will hear the words 'Off home early, then?' followed by a mumbled 'Yah – well – I've put in a lot of office lunches and Saturdays lately' or a deceitful 'Got to go up to Production for an hour. I just thought I'd take my coat to, um, save time later.' You may then imagine the scornful curl of the lip with which the saintly figure at the desk greets this. Even though it might be perfectly true about the working lunches; and even though the assailant may be on fixed hours and be the kind of paranoid clockwatcher who won't pick up a phone at 1.59 if his lunchbreak lasts till two. Despite all this, the barb sticks. In offices which open six or seven days a week – like newspapers – some men who wish to signal that they are working outside their allocated hours go to the desperate lengths of appearing in the office in a fluffy pullover instead of a jacket on Saturdays. They might as well have someone knit the words MY DAY OFF onto the chest and have done with it.

But if some flexible workers do suffer from the 'Off home early, then?' form of harassment, possibly they should examine their consciences. Have they never done the opposite? Floated past a preoccupied (usually female) colleague at 5.30 and said: 'You work too hard, sweetheart! There are other things in life, you know'? This – with its subtext implying that one has no friends or invitations, and ends the day watching Blind Date in a lonely little flat – is possibly the world's most annoying remark. Especially when what you are doing is, come to think of it, supposed to be his job too.

But by the time you whirl your chair round to say so, however, the swine will have vanished down the staircase for the night leaving only a whiff of Eau Sauvage. I suppose you could always stick your head out of the window and shout 'OFF HOME EARLY, THEN?' But he might not hear.

2

Training pains

I had a glamorous college friend once who couldn't afford driving
lessons. Having a first-class mind, she hit upon the brilliant idea
of joining the University Officer Training Corps, who undertook to
teach new recruits to drive free. They were operating a strenuous,
almost desperate, equal-opportunities policy at the time and wel-
comed anything female with open arms: so she got in, and after a
few enjoyable weeks of grinding the gears on an armoured Ferret,
passed the test. The Army, poor innocents, were pleased with their
investment: they clearly saw her as a most presentable WRAC driver
or the kind of gorgeous Reservist they could put on posters. My
friend intended, as she always had, to resign instantly.

But conscience intervened. She couldn't bring herself to do it. For
weeks she lingered on with the OTC, vowing at least to stick with
them until the Remembrance Sunday parade. I shall never forget
the struggle we had on the big day, to get her, half-hysterical,
into her puttees or gaiters or whatever they were called, while
she muttered 'one-two, right wheel' to herself. She marched, with
a noticeable Vogue-ish catwalk sway, then went to the CO and
did the dreadful treacherous deed. Driving made her feel guilty
for ages.

I am grateful to the Employment Secretary for this trip down
memory lane. This week a White Paper (as white and woolly
indeed as a newborn lamb) proposed that the Government may
consider 'clarifying' the law on training contracts: thus enabling
employers to get some money back when expensively trained staff

leave prematurely. The employee might pay, or there might be a transfer fee from the poaching company.

The trouble is that it is not always a matter of poaching. Some training programmes are deliberately designed to weed people out. I am told by coweringly anonymous insiders that if you make it through a Marks & Spencer management course you will make it through anything up to and including World War III. Young policemen at Hendon (don't be fooled by their rather sweet Miss-World type sashes and fresh faces) are being tested as much as trained. Unfortunately the weeding process sometimes doesn't take effect until the last day, because the victim has determined to show the bastards: does Mr Howard intend to recoup training costs from newly unemployed victims? Shame! They haven't got any money, anyway: I know one boy who went through three weeks of intensive sales training (residential, 15 hours a day including 'brain-gym' groups and chants), came home, resigned and spent two weeks in bed.

One American company did set up a training contact for its British arm: trainees had to pay £4,000 compensation if they stayed less than two years. This fell to pieces when a large group dived for freedom all at once, depositing £100 each with a lawyer to fight their case if necessary. The ones I know have not paid a penny more. Ironically, one of the reasons they left was that they didn't want to belong to an organization which was mistrustful enough of its own appeal to bind its staff with fiscal blackmail (it is blackmail: what normal 22-year-old has got £4,000 or a lawyer?).

One can see the companies' point. A trained sheepdog is worth more than an untrained one and the same goes for people. If the difference in value is showing as a red hole in your budget, you feel cross. And there are a few serious time-wasters around who just adore being trained: it is a bit like the Munchausen's Syndrome which takes healthy people into hospital time after time. I remember when adult retraining first took off, several women – lazy wives of wealthy men – took free secretarial courses although they had no intention of ever wasting good shopping-time in an office. 'Ay'm doing it to find myself,' said one smugly. Puritanism reared within me, and I told her she ought to be had up for wasting public money.

But would the system work both ways? Has Mr Howard

considered the fact that some in-service training is now so potty that it probably reduces your employability? All those leadership courses may turn out leaders, but they also quite unnecessarily reveal flaws. Can a chap sue for loss of future earnings and credibility if the management forces him to walk up Helvellyn, sleep in a plastic bag, put on a pantomime within half-a-day and admit in front of the whole Marketing department that he is frightened of spiders? Or if he gets so emotionally bonded to the rest of his Group (after the night in the plastic bag) that he dare not take up better offers for fear of trauma?

Come to that, can I demand compensation from Condé Nast for once sending me to a Magazine Editors' Seminar which has prevented me from ever again taking the world of glossy magazines remotely seriously? And where, moreover, Maggie Goodman (now editor of *Hello!*) gave such a moving speech on the need for 'white space' in one's diary that I have barely made a single entry since, and never know where I am meant to be?

3

Not that kind of girl

Londlon licensed taxi drivers have had a nasty week. The arrest of a man for one of the alleged black-cab rapes has helped, but the 'Ride to terror' headlines and the outbreak of doomy articles by women who no longer feel safe about cabs has shaken the trade up badly. Through last week there were great lunch-hour meetings, cryptic radio conversations, and tirades at passengers about the drivers' passionate commitment to helping the police. A whole trade, a whole culture, had been smirched: the wound went a lot deeper than their pockets, even in these lean times. It was a matter of a blot on the escutcheon. Of course, the cabbies all know perfectly well that even the most vociferous scaremongers will come back, because most women know that most cabbies are chivalrous to a fault and more likely to drive off their assailants with a starting-handle than to harass them with so much as an improper wink. It is the loss of corporate pride that rankles.

It set me thinking about other professions which have gone through patches of bad press, and what the individual's strategy for survival might be. The 'one-bad-apple' line of defence used to be much favoured by the police force back in Dixon days, but after the Guildford, Birmingham and Tottenham appeals, and the shaming Stefan Kiszko case in which nobody quite knows who 'lost' the sample that would have saved a man sixteen years in jail, decent policemen everywhere must be squirming. Being in a smirched profession is awful, and the more innocent you are personally, the worse it is. We invest so much of ourselves in our jobs that to have them fall victim to a blanket condemnation is almost like being at the receiving end of racist taunts: I shall never forget one young man who earnestly said to me in the flower power sixties, 'I'm in the army, but I'm not like that really.' And one can see the rationale of the old BBC guidelines which thundered against any behaviour, in or out of the studios, which tended to 'bring the Name of the Corporation into Disrepute'. The phrase used to make me tremble when I was a trainee: one felt that one incautious oath when one trod in a dog-mess during a tricky Outside Broadcast could bring the whole baroque structure tumbling ruinously about one's ears.

No ancient and dignified profession is entirely free from risk. Ask any teacher. During the strikes of the mid-1980s, it was not only the militants who suffered. One mild primary school headmistress from Oxfordshire, who I suspect has never voted farther left than Douglas Hurd, was taking a class on a trip to a London museum. Quite gratuitously, a middle-aged woman glanced at the book she was reading (while the well-behaved children chattered and looked out of the train window) and hissed 'Marx, I suppose! *Teachers!*' That was extreme, but others can tell you of the sidelong glances, the sudden frosty reserve which followed them during those years. Even today a few are tempted to walk around wearing badges saying I TEACH PHONICS AND USE A BLACKBOARD, OK? Similarly, the Natural Childbirth movement made it unsafe to admit that one was a consultant obstetrician: 'Hah!' young women would say aggressively, 'I suppose you're one of the forceps-and-stirrups brigade.' Hard to digest your canapés after that.

Some jobs, of course, have chronic spiritual halitosis as far as the public are concerned. I suppose their practitioners learn to live with it. They can't plead the 'few bad apples' defence, so are left with the option of either deciding that they are, personally, the only good apple, or else believing passionately that they are very useful and the public are ignorant swine. Traffic wardens can be observed doing both alternately: beaming helpfully at old ladies on crossings one minute, and sanctimoniously lecturing a harassed mother on the wickedness of having a three-day-overdue tax disc the next. It must be confusing for them.

Tax inspectors? The only one I ever knew socially was a cheerful chap, full of funny, if alarming, stories. Colleagues, he admitted, were less upfront. At parties they tend to pretend they are actuaries or (in one case) a North Sea rig diver – 'it makes him feel good to say that'. Oddly, I knew a social worker who told the same lie. Divers are obviously a safe disguise, since whatever they do is brave, incomprehensible, and takes place far up north and well underwater.

Unlike the calling of estate agents, which is right up everyone's street (and, indeed, nose). They went through the fire of unpopularity when the house price boom turned to total slump overnight and we all needed someone to bash. There are glimmers of returning sympathy now, but meanwhile, one confessed, the knack of being in an unpopular trade is 'to know worse jokes about your profession than anyone else does. Why do estate agents never look out of the window in the morning? So they'll have something to do in the afternoon.'

Politicians and journalists always seem to score the lowest rating. I used to believe that I spoke to my children in moderate and optimistic terms about our democratic processes. But when my infant wandered in to see Parliament on TV and innocently asked, 'Which ones are the bastards, Mummy?' I realized that the odd prejudice might have slipped my guard.

But as a journalist, I am a victim too. I once asked an upright lady JP to sign our passport photographs (the form demanded a citizen of standing: doctor, teacher, councillor etc.). 'The trouble is,' I said, 'they don't seem to count journalists as respectable citizens!' It was a joke. Not to her, though. With a serious JP glance, she replied 'Well, that's right. You can't wonder, can you?' Speechless, I groped for names to confound her, for James Cameron, Robert Fox, for Allsops and Dimblebys and Levins and Mulchrones, but no words came. In her view, we were all down there in the gutter scrawling 'ELVIS WAS A WEREWOLF' or 'SEX CHANGE EXPERTS' MIDNIGHT RUSH TO PALACE'.

Ooh, just let her wait. There'll be a scandal about magistrates soon, and I shall point, and jeer.

4

Keeping up

*T*wo old TV lags were sitting the other day having their make-up plastered on for an afternoon's hard smiling, when their eyes fell on a discarded Times Business Section. Grim initials faced them: HDTV. It could only mean one thing: trembling, they read on. High Definition Television, said the piece, may begin experimentally by mid-1992.

The pair – a man and woman, both in that well-preserved early middle age which passes for youth on prime-time TV – looked at one another sadly. After years of late nights, parenthood and piquant little Australian supermarket clarets, each had to admit that the thing attached to the front of his or her head was unmistakeably a Low-Definition face. Any improvement in man's technical ability to broadcast detailed pictures was clearly going to spell Kismet for both of them. Or, at the very least, a serious falling-off in the postal proposals of marriage by which media personalities are inclined to measure their popular appeal. Technology had struck again.

Its forward march is always a mixed blessing for those who are nicely dug in to the world as it is. Few of us do our jobs only because of their end-product. Rather, we tend to find that we happen to suit the way in which the job gets done. Human beings can develop an almost marital affection for the tools and appurtenances of their trade. Mechanical engineers visibly enjoy oily rags, and pistons, and machine-tools. Sound mixers in recording studios affectionately slide the faders up and down, and have their favourite decks even among identical models. Electricians actually like wire, writers like clean symmetrical stacks of typescript, and – before those machines were cruelly snatched away – secretaries used to know the 'ping!' of their own typewriter's carriage-return as a mahout knows his favourite elephant's footstep. And it goes further than that: the rituals and ways of operation within an organization get a terrible grip on you, too. 'The Ten O'Clock Monday Meeting' becomes as comfortingly familiar as Evensong in the Cathedral Close: if some business-school iconoclast turns up and moves it to Tuesday at 4 o'clock everyone feels miserable and dispossessed. Put the chairs in a square instead of a semicircle and they'll probably go off sick.

So when the landscape of a job changes all is panic. Office managers, during the first mass switch to word-processors, frequently had to ban dissident staff from smuggling in old upright Remingtons. In Accounts, determined employees called themselves 'bookkeepers' long after the last book had been transformed into a collection of shimmering bytes.

But at least the job was basically unchanged. I used to know a signalman on the Oxford line, who lived a happy life in a white clapboard signal-box, among big brass levers which he polished daily. He had a window looking out on the trains, a pot plant, and a kettle to make his cup of tea in between the 10.43 and the 11.16. His kingdom was neat and shipshape and personal, his efficiency unquestioned.

Then they computerized the signals. He showed me the new box, a cubbyhole of green, winking lights and neat little buttons over which his great polisher's paw hovered incongruously. 'I'm off,' he said. 'It's a toy for computer-mad kids now. Not a man's job.' Indeed railwaymen and heavy engineers have probably had more heartbreak in that way than most. If you spent your youth making steam-engines to last a hundred years, it is terrible to end up bolting together tumble-driers.

Down the road from us in Leiston there used to operate the distinguished old firm of Garrett's Engineering. They built steam-engines, locomotives, everything. If you go far enough up the Amazon today, you will find some faithful old Garrett engine still wheezing away, powering a sawmill or pumping water. After the age of steam the firm tried to change: men who had served loving apprenticeships on the big, proud, everlasting steam-engines found themselves putting together tinny modern tumble-driers. In the end it closed. It is only a few professions, like acting, where technical progress can be defied by people who like doing things the old way. Live theatre exists now in Britain solely because actors like doing it. They like to perform plays in the right order, without retakes, and to feel an audience breathing. So – like Juliet Stevenson, turning down Hollywood to take the Equity minimum at the Royal Court for *Death and the Maiden* – they are prepared to do it for a tenth the rate they could get on film or television.

Not only technology changes jobs: ideology does it too. How often have you seen someone dive for early retirement because it's 'no job for a gentleman any more'? Or because women have come in and spoiled everything? Last week there was a failed case for sexual discrimination, wherein Ms Nadine Gardiner-Rosse was sacked for refusing to attend a client's motivation meetings which were coarse, sexist and in admitted bad taste. We were all meant to feel sorry for her. And so we did. But perversely, a corner of my sympathies crept across to the chaps who held the meetings and felt that she shouldn't have minded ('The black office boy,' someone incredibly said, 'didn't mind being called Sambo'). Poor old dinosaurs: they had clearly been foul-mouthing and nudging their way through business life for years, until civilization suddenly roared past and left them blinking stupidly.

Perhaps the most admirable of us are those who happily discard a whole life's disciplines to give the new order a whirl. I went back to my old school after ten years and met my history teacher, an angular earnest woman permanently fifty-five years old. She greeted me with a cheerful 'Hello. I taught you terribly badly, you know. I was doing it all wrong in those days. I've been on some courses and I do it much better now. Quite different.' What a heroine.

5

In praise of tips

*E*very now and again, as predictable as rain in springtime, there arises in Britain an agonized, embarrassed, puritanical debate on the subject of tipping. I don't know any other nation that worries so much on the subject of gratuities – to waiters, waitresses, taxi-drivers, porters, maids, or whoever. The debate takes place between those who feel it exploits the tipper, those who fear that it degrades the tippee, and those who have no objection in principle but just find it terribly, terribly embarrassing and never know how much to give.

The argument is now rearing its head again: encouraged by the defeatist habit adopted by so many catering establishments of pre-empting the tip altogether with a 10 or 15 per cent service charge automatically added to the bill. These charges annoy a lot of people, and in a recent report the Consumers Association said, with its usual plain-spoken Nonconformist tidy-mindedness, that routine service charges should be abolished. If food costs more, then it costs more, so the argument goes: there shouldn't be a notional extra charge for putting it on the plate.

It was noticeable, though, that even the Consumers Association – the high priests of commercial decorum, predictable prices and consumer rights – did not quite dare to go to the extreme and condemn tipping altogether. The report admitted that consumers need 'the option to tip in appreciation of exceptional service'.

But I say never mind their needs: think about the waiter's. It is unfortunate that all the arguments about tipping always seem to come from customers. We rarely hear from those who rake in the gratuities, possibly because none of them are journalists. Nobody tips journalists, more's the pity: speaking for myself it would brighten up my day considerably if a grateful editor were to wink lasciviously and tuck a tenner down my cleavage. Of course, in the old free-spending days before unsmiling accountants took over Fleet Street, some travelling reporters used to take the responsibility of tipping themselves with their proprietor's money, noting the sum down on the expenses sheet as 'sundries' or 'hire of camel', or 'lunch with confidential MI5 contact'. But even this form of self-righteous cheating can never have been quite the same as a real tip. A tip comes out of the blue: it is a joyful bonus, a shot in the arm, a small adventure. I tell you, I have been a waitress and a barmaid and a tourist guide, and I know about these things. And never mind embarrassment, never mind degradation, or the myriad boringly niggling nuances of the British class system. I will tell you a bald and rarely stated truth: people who get tips LIKE GETTING THEM. Large or small, it does not matter. They make you feel extremely good.

Of course, what I say is heresy to the politically correct modern liberal. Being a well-organized wage slave himself, he considers tipping to be awfully demeaning and embarrassing. He goes through agonies of fear that he is patronizing the waiter or taxi-driver: as if giving a man money meant you assume yourself better than him. This chap's arrival in a hotel is absolutely ruined for him by the need to grope surreptitiously in his pocket for what he calculates as the right amount to give the porter who takes his luggage up: his misery has been compounded by the arrival of the new pound coins, because he has a vague feeling that it is more insulting – more primitive somehow – to give a person coins than to hand over a note. He can't concentrate on the pleasure of the hotel, the affability of the porter, the sight of his room overlooking the ocean and the sunset: until this poor sap hands over the tip and gets rid of the porter he is an emotional cripple, mentally doubled up with the anguish of embarrassment.

But what is going on in this worried liberal's mind is a quite misguided attempt at empathy. He is not a waiter, or a porter, or a guide, or a maid: he is an office worker, or a banker, or a doctor or teacher. And he is imagining how HE would cringe with humiliation if his income were to arrive in any other way than a discreet monthly banker's order, siphoning the money invisibly into his bank. This chap is not at all mean: he gives to charity and campaigns for national minimum wages and wants to pay more tax. What frets him so much is the randomness of tipping: the fact that it is personal, unstructured, and that there are no firm rules to follow.

But that is his nature, and he can't help it. There are people who tip openly and handsomely and with a conspiratorial wink: they are of quite a different type. They are business buccaneers, rascals, wide boys, chancers. They don't worry about whether they are degrading people by tipping them. Oh no. They don't think money is degrading: they think it is pretty good fun, and cannot imagine how anybody could mind having a bit more of it. So the message they convey as they proffer a fiver and a grin is, 'I've had a bit of luck today, darling, now here's yours.' And you, the waitress, tuck the fiver into your apron pocket and grin back, conveying the silent message, 'Good on you, mate. Keep it up.' And you barely give a glance to the worried liberal on the corner table, who meanwhile is sorting through his change-purse trying to calculate a precise 12½ per cent and muttering, 'If they paid these people properly there'd be no need for this.' When he gives you the money he won't even smile. Well really, who would you prefer to deal with?

Anyway, he's wrong about there being no need for tips if people are paid properly. What the jolly buccaneer knows and the anxious liberal does not is that if you are doing a rather dreary, mundane daily job, the thing that lifts your spirit is a bit of unpredictability. An adventure. When I was dragging tourists round Oxford it was not only profitable but a source of endless interest and entertainment to be able to say, 'Had a good day, thank God for Texans!' or 'Do you know those Danes tipped me in Kroner because they'd run out of sterling, and I've just looked up the exchange rate and it's nearly twenty quid! God bless them.' When I was pulling pints and lugging crates of beer around in an Irish bar, for a very basic wage indeed, it buoyed me up to think, 'Aha, I beat the average this week, thanks to that drunk judge from Dublin! I wonder whether it really was his daughter?' And it wasn't all down to sheer luck, either: in those days I could do a particularly good trick with flying beermats which sometimes earned me the price of four or five drinks from admiring audiences. Not entirely unaffected by the best Jamiesons whiskey, they would say, 'That's amazing, have-one-yourself-darling.' And I would raise my glass, and pocket the money. (A barmaid, as you know, keeps a glass of soda-water always at the ready to raise courteously to the gent who thinks he has bought her a gin.)

Of course, nobody likes the idea of forcing a free man or woman to rely on tips for a living wage, as a beggar does. But if a bearable minimum is guaranteed by one's employer, there is no doubt that tips improve the day. London taxi-drivers, in my experience, heartily agree. They have a reputation for surliness, but get them talking about Great Tips they have known and they are full of boyish enthusiasm. 'It gives you an interest,' said one. 'You lay bets with yourself who'll do you best. The amazing thing is it's often the scruffiest people who give the best tips.' Although taxi-drivers rely on tips, and indeed need them, because the Inland Revenue taxes them on a notional proportion of their take, they are not entirely mercenary: that spirit of adventure and unpredictability still counts for a good deal. Most drivers tell with relish stories of small but significant tips, like the old lady who gave one a box of Turkish Delight from her shopping bag because he said he had children; and numbers of cab drivers generously reversed the tipping process by giving free rides at the height of the Robert Maxwell pension scandal to those of his former employees who went around London with ironically jokey buttons saying MAXWELL PENSIONER PLEASE GIVE GENEROUSLY. But it must be admitted that all taxi-drivers seem to remember with wistfulness, above all, the days of the City Big Bang in the late 1980s, when the new breed of barrow-boy dealers felt seriously rich and expressed their exuberance with folding money.

Those dealers, of course, were on a similar exhilarating roller-coaster themselves. They would win massive commissions one day and nothing the next, which if you think about it made them kindred spirits of those whom they tipped. And – forgetting the poor wet guilty liberal wage-slave I depicted before – a lot of us are like that. We may wear white collars, but the old primitive needs drive us. We all came out of the jungle, and not all of us, even in our regimented society, have managed to bury the hunting instinct under a mound of Monthly Budget Accounts and automatic salary increments. There is still a powerful drive to stalk our prey, pounce, gorge and then starve until the next kill because we know deep down, in our jungly hearts, that that is the way life is. A matter of ups and downs, not a gentle predictable ascent to a restful plateau. At the extreme, to make life more exciting we go freelance. More moderate spirits stick with a salaried job for safety, but still revel in tips, and bonuses and commissions and windfalls.

Everywhere you look in ordinary lives – even in over-organized, salaried, pensioned, welfare-cushioned Western industrialized nations – you find echoes of the old instinct to hunt and deal and bargain and pull stunts. Reflections of the jungle and the souk. Eighteenth-century British naval captains were allowed to supplement their pay by capturing the odd French ship on their own initiative; modern British MPs capture directorships and lecture tours. The sagest, most dignified of newspaper writers positively twinkle with glee when the BBC invites them on to a radio or television programme, be it serious discussion or frivolous quiz. It is not only the chance to show off that pleases, but the fact that it is quite fun to be, as it were, tipped sixty quid on top of one's routine pay. Examples are everywhere: a senior BBC editor used to bring eggs into the office from his smallholding and sell them across his desk, counting the pennies with glee. A decorous solicitor in Lincolnshire likes nothing more than to go Morris-dancing round the pubs at weekends, and pass the hat. My own husband is a television and newspaper journalist, but also rears pigs on our small farm and gets his biggest kicks out of selling pork chops at the farm gate for a fraction of the profit he gets from his mainstream work. Middle-aged secretaries go home to a vivid life of secret buccaneering enterprise, selling soft toys or Tupperware: a school headmistress recently was discovered by the local paper to have a second string as an exotic dancer in night-clubs, wearing nothing but a sequinned bikini and a tame python. And even when people do these extra, moneyspinning, tip-attracting activities for charity, the same buzz is present. Anyone who has ever watched a Mother Teresa of Calcutta bazaar committee counting the take will know how gleeful they are, how competitive and critical: not so much like a group of middle-aged ladies organizing a jumble sale, as a pride of lionesses raking over the day's kill.

And why not? After all, who was it who outlawed the rakish pursuits of tipping and private trading? The old communist bloc, where every other fine eccentric flowering of the human spirit was stamped upon, too. So don't be embarrassed, next time an occasion of tipping comes your way. Give the man a quid. With a flourish. And if you can, for heaven's sake try to wink.

6

The unknown commuter

*W*e are now approaching the broad sunlit uplands, where a brave and prosperous new Britain will stride into the dawn of the European millennium. It must be true: ever since last Thursday, various plausible gents in different coloured rosettes have been telling me so. And who am I to doubt that one of them will shortly deliver the goods?

In this new age, terrorism will wither and die and our cities be revitalized. There will be supertrains and electric buses and clean new piazzas and boulevards where fountains play and the Prince of Wales nods approvingly from behind a Doric column.

So I have a proposal. A fine country needs fine statuary, and it also needs reminding of the bad old days from which it has struggled free. Why else did the communist bloc adorn itself so lavishly with images of worker-heroes breaking their chains and waving picks at the rising sun? Imperial countries prefer military figures, preferably with breeches and tricorne hats, and religious countries appreciate saints at their street-corners: but for Britain's future there is only one symbolic figure worth putting on a plinth. We must erect, at each quadrant of the capital city, a twenty-foot-high granite memorial to the Unknown Commuter.

He – or perhaps she – will carry a briefcase, but the right arm will be upflung, shading the eyes as if looking for an impossible bus. The stance will be heroic, the gaze stern and unwavering. Perhaps in the Commuter's teeth there may be a dog-eared ticket; or perhaps it lies discarded at his feet, as if he had just accepted that there is no way that the system is going to get him any further than East Croydon before noon. The statues – one at Stratford East, one at Clapham Junction, and so on – will remind the prosperous children of the millennium what a hard road their forefathers trod. They will shed a tear at the thought of those brave journeys recounted in ballad and song: those six-hour marathons, those heartbreaks at Shenfield and dark nights of the soul just outside London Bridge. Perhaps they will murmur 'Never again!' as they throw posies at our scuffed granite toecaps.

Commuters are the undoubted heroes of our time. In their dogged, chirpy endurance they are the true heirs of the men who won the war. (Actually, a few of the older faces on the 7.47 are the same ones who did win the war: there was a treasurable moment at a public meeting in Ipswich a few years ago when an elderly man – on being told that only 9 of the 18 locomotives were operational because they were 'very complicated pieces of machinery' – announced that he used to supervise the maintenance of 18 equally complicated Lancaster bombers. 'And if I'd ever had fewer than sixteen fit to fly to Germany, I'd have lost my job.' Gales of bitter laughter.)

The commuter is rarely praised. But who else keeps the wheels of commerce turning through strikes and snow, leaves on the points and persons on the track? Through crashes and bombs and rumours of bombs? The commuter's determination is legendary, his – and her – patience superhuman. On the rare occasions when a few rebel and do something feisty like getting out and walking along the tracks because nobody will tell them anything, they are loftily condemned as irresponsible; yet on the thousand other days when they meekly put up with the unbearable, nobody says a kind word. It is time for statuary.

Not of me, I hasten to· add. Not any more. As a Greenwich rail commuter while the Dartford Guards were going through a particularly impetuous phase, I know what it is to trudge through Deptford in the sleet in order to steam myself dry against some stranger's hot bomber-jacket on the East London line. But since we moved farther afield I only travel once or twice a week. I am a mere amateur. But I have my moments: leaving the car in Golders Green during the summer rail-and-tube strikes in order to ride a bendy folding bicycle down to Broadcasting House, yomping through snowdrifts, practising Zen meditation for hours outside Witham. Last week, in the Budget Day bomb scares, I was offloaded at Ilford instead of Liverpool Street with no trains likely for three hours. Luckily I was in company with my big brother Mike, a toughened commuter, and with half-mile bus queues in every direction and a disinclination to stand in the station with all the other extras from Dante's *Inferno* ('So many . . . I had not known death had undone so many . . .') we decided to walk out into the swirling grit and drizzle like Captain Oates and take our chance. Behind us trailed a few other business suits with the same quixotic resolve, and we heard their hollow laughter echoing ours as we trudged through the blighted urban wilderness breathing lead and reading signs thanking us for visiting Ilford. We completed our five-hour journey some time later in a crawling taxi with two affable and resigned bankers. Not one of us burst into tears.

Commuters are good at what psychologists call Coping Strategies. Some stay wry and resigned, like the old stager who once told my brother, 'Don't ever let it get to you. I've watched men grow old in front of my eyes that way.' Others, like his friend Harry, exorcize the blue-devils with a flamboyant stroppiness. Once he was left so long on a freezing platform that he refused to show the guard his ticket, claiming his hands were too cold to find it. 'In my pocket somewhere. Welcome to rummage. You find it,' he told a baffled conductor. Another time a Panda car called to warn him off for threatened mayhem at Farringdon and found that this was the very man they had been warning off at London Bridge earlier in the evening. They remembered telling him to 'Try Farringdon, Sir.'

Together with nunlike self-discipline, the good commuter has the resourcefulness of a backpacker. Look around a delayed train and hardly anybody fumes: instead they take out poker-dice and Penguin Classics, practise isometric exercises or fall asleep. When the lights go out they produce torches and candle-lanterns. They know how to feed the spirit, too. One legendary passenger on the Norwich line always carries a copy of the baroque Conditions of Carriage and studies them ostentatiously. He has discovered an ancient law that 'no passenger may operate any valve, lever, switch or mechanical device save those controlling heating and lighting', and never tires of pointing out that this makes it illegal to flush the lavatory. Don't tell me he doesn't deserve a statue.

29

7

Take a break

*T*hose who are alert to the fine nuances of Radio 4 will have noticed that I am not Jonathan Dimbleby. More precisely, that there has been an interruption in my normal practice of going vocal on Wednesday mornings to solicit the life-stories and philosophies of the great, the good and the just plain odd. Studio B14 is strangely silent, bereft of its floating population of actors, survivors, mavericks, geniuses, strip artistes, collectors of Malagasy hissing cockroaches and players upon exotic musical instruments. For Midweek is off the air: replaced in the interests of the democratic process by Election Call. If they so wish the mavericks, geniuses, strippers and cockroach fanciers may phone up and harass captive politicians instead.

As, indeed, may I. There is an odd mixture of thrill and dismay about an unexpected month of paid furlough. A hole yawns in the middle of the week. There are tasks to fill it, of course, most of them woefully overdue. All freelance writers live with guilt: sometimes, on spotting a particular publisher's editor at a party, I have been reduced to dropping on all fours behind the nearest sofa and crawling away rather than meet those reproachful eyes. But nonetheless there is a brief sense of stolen leisure.

Naturally, I have used it. I put in some heavy training on cup-cakes for my role as second anchor in the Middleton Ladies' Tug-o'-War team (we beat Westleton, thank you. Hauled 'em off their feet). I have fitted in a couple of days flu, during which I fell asleep during PM and woke up at the end of The Archers feverishly and tearfully convinced that Paddy Ashdown was being forced to have his Middle White sow Freda put down because of the Labour Budget. I tried tidying my desk, but stopped because whenever I open the drawerful of old work I start reading it and trying to work out when my heyday was, or whether I ever had one, which leads to maudlin drinking.

Most of all, tiny and finite though my own lay-off is, I have been brooding about all those others who find themselves paid not to go to work. Like doctors under investigation: the other week we heard that in the past six years some seventy senior doctors have been suspended with pay and that there are at least nineteen hanging around at this very moment waiting for a verdict to lift them out of limbo. Or teachers: the NUT couldn't say how many exist in similar suspension, but anecdotal evidence suggests quite a few. Nor does anyone seem to tot up the number of police, clergy, or lawyers in that state.

The secret idlers of industry are even more hard to number. Straw-polling, though, quickly revealed an engineer suspected of taking bribes (and later cleared) who built his neighbour a 15 ft tall rockery during his five-months' layoff, and a managing director whose whole company was whisked from under him in a corporate shake-up, but whose contract debars him from working for anyone else for a year. He is irritating his family by making flow charts of their daily activities. And in this profession we have one of the most famous examples of all. Times Newspapers' staff journalists, who were paid for over a year during the print strike to produce no newspapers. If you are tempted to think it was fun, hear a veteran like Philip Howard: he offers a sad little portrait of their day. 'We would come to work out of habit, have a news conference, pass on the gossip and then drift off to the pub. Then we drifted rather sadly home again.' At least they could gather round the old tribal fire together: unlike the suspended copper barred from the station, the teacher deprived of children. It hardly bears thinking of.

But what do you do all day, when you are salaried but unemployed? Apart, that is, from worry about the doom of disgrace or redundancy which might follow? Since the prime cure for worry is work, such suffering should not be treated lightly. But the fact remains that from day to day, one must *do* something. Some write books or moonlight, but on the whole suspendees are probably best occupied in completely different jobs. These provide both a challenge and a bracing symbolic two fingers to your real profession. Like the policeman who devoted his limbo to fitting out a steel yacht. The idea was to sail away quick if the inquiry found against him: it didn't, and he sold the boat. The buyer tells me that bits kept falling off it: presumably the ones screwed on during particularly black moments of self-doubt.

Philip Howard of *The Times* became a butler – an inspired choice, since literary editors and Jeeveses require similar gravitas and eyebrow-lifting skills. 'I was a good butler,' he recalls with simple pride, 'I once served a buffet supper for a thousand gynaecologists, and the Queen.'

Now there's a thought. Let it be known that I am available, in black dress and frilly apron, for functions on the next three Tuesday evenings. Turn up your collars, diners, and beware the flying scampi. After twenty years safely immured in white-collar occupations, the World's Worst Waitress walks again.

8

Pitching

*A*pril has sprung, and any day now my friend Barry will be off on
his rounds again. He sells swimming-pools, and the first watery
rays of spring sunlight start his telephone ringing as if by solar
power. Between now and June he will quarter the countryside with
his trusty carphone at his side, calling as requested on ambitious
householders. He will unfold brochures about expandable liners;
he will prod the soil, narrow his eyes, take copious measurements
and say: 'Did you want the spoil landscaping?' Finally he will hand
over a video of consenting couples in tracksuits indulging in DIY
grouting. He will do this five times a day with a straight face, before
going home to write out estimates.

Take off your hat to him, for the man deserves an Oscar. All the
time he is discussing silica sand filters, Barry knows in his heart
that most of these punters are pure fantasists, as likely to order a
Lear-jet as a swimming-pool. Some of them call him out year after
year with different schemes to waste his time: now musing on a
marble pool in the rose-garden, now toying with a solar-heated
conservatory jacuzzi. Barry keeps on smiling and estimating, just
in case. You never know.

Estimates, pitches, presentations, auditions, pilot programmes:
most trades contain an element of casting your bread upon the
waters and watching it float away. I say trades, because the
professions tend to weasel out of it: when did you last get
rival solicitors to estimate their costs, or rival doctors pitching
for the contract to do your BUPA cartilage? Even estate agents

have started covering themselves against failure by charging an extra fee for producing details of your house even if they never sell it.

But honest trades almost always have to pitch, estimate, or audition for work. And a heartbreaking business it is. What hell to be an architect in competition (do they get paid for those dinky models? Do they smash them in fury when they fail?). Pity the torment of the unpublished author, but pity also the advertising account manager who works night and day on a super new way to sell spaghetti hoops, and whose artful structure of smoked-salmon buffets, storyboards and smiling girls with big hair is kicked down in ten minutes. Weep for the independent TV producer who spends weeks clipping together snazzy bits of desktop publishing complete with imitation preview cuttings from imaginary newspapers, all for some whey-faced mandarin to sneer at. Some producers actually research a whole, real, set of willing film subjects for their proposal even though those actual people will be well over their plastic surgery before the money comes through, so the work will have to be done over again. It doesn't matter. The customer is always right, the swine.

What does this endless pitching do to the human soul? Psychologists, never having had to audition themselves, tend to concentrate on the warping effects of sexual rejection or being ripped untimely from the maternal breast. They never give a thought to the equally cruel, routine rejection of one's work. For estimates *are* work. Barry might do a brilliant offer, cutting the pipework costs by a cunning detour under the garage and throwing in a free inflatable crocodile: only to be totally ignored. An actor may vainly work all week on an audition, a salesman produce a customized proposal, or a copywriter put her whole soul into a new way of telling the aspirational AB woman that Renaults make your heels grow higher. All for nothing.

I once had a flirtation with the world of commercial voiceovers. They shut me up in a cellar in Soho for two full hours and made me intone 'Natural Choice – it's the *natural* choice' in a thousand different voices ('Could you put more warmth into the *choice*, lovey? Think nuts, think furry squirrels!'). Drained and ashamed, I went home only to be told a week later that 'The client's decided to go with Richard Briers.' I snarled that I hoped they would be very happy together, and vowed to stick to honest toil. The following week a magazine asked for a 500-word synopsis and then lost it; and the BBC – having made me do a pilot programme (pretty naff, actually) kept a nine-month silence and then without a word opened the series with Another Woman presenting it. She even used one of my jokes. And was there an NHS Rejection Therapist to turn to? There was not.

At least if you have estimated, auditioned or posted an unsolicited manuscript, you have had time to prepare for failure. Even worse is the poisonous showbiz practice of the Availability Check. This involves a brisk woman ringing you up and asking if you are interested in going to the Seychelles for a week's filming, starring in the Amazing Technicolour Dreamcoat, guesting for Edna Everage or undergoing some similar life-transforming experience. She will be most insistent that you 'pencil it in' and keep the dates free. Chat-show researchers then spend an hour asking your opinion on everything from incest to City fraud. Then silence. Ring back and she will say that the client loved the idea, only Richard Briers came free . . .

Don't do it. Unavailability Is Strength. Or if you do pencil it in, just don't order a swimming-pool from Barry on the strength of it.

9

Psychotribology

I think I have found a new career. More than found one: I will have founded it. I am going to set up as the world's first consultant psychotribologist.

If you are a good solid back-page reader, you are already a jump ahead of me, crying 'Yes! We need psychotribology now!' Last week *The Times* introduced plain tribology to a wider public on the occasion of the Institution of Mechanical Engineers' new War on Wear campaign. The word comes from the Greek *tribein*, meaning 'to rub', and is the study of things which rub against each other, which grind and squeak at one another's hostile surfaces and throw off shavings of swarf. If we could lubricate them better we would save energy, prevent mechanical breakdown and be £1.5 billion a year richer. China did a study and found that over 1.8 per cent of its national income was being wasted on useless rubbing. So that's tribology: oiling the wheels of industry.

And psychotribology? Well, you know already. Just look around you, at the way your colleague on the left keeps sniffing at his Vick inhaler, and the one on the right is rearranging her drawerful of neat little paisley-patterned boxes marked PAPERCLIPS and PERSONAL. Psychotribology has to come. After all, if £1.5 billion a year is being lost through squeaky ball-bearings and incompatible cogs, how much more is being wasted on the capacity of human workmates to rub each other up the wrong way, present jagged and damaging surfaces, and generally get up one another's noses?

What is the point of installing an expensive new executive, finely engineered at INSEAD and Harvard Business School, if he is going to waste half his energy grinding horribly against the rough surfaces of his ex-works 'basically, I'm a barrer-boy' Managing Director? Why take such trouble fining down and polishing job-descriptions for a new PA, only to offer her up to a departmental head with a personality like coarse sandpaper and a work pattern designed by a committee of Heath Robinson and Jeffrey Bernard? On the other hand, why waste your time on an anti-harassment code if the tolerances of your employees are all equally crude, and the girls fouler-mouthed cogs than the boys?

Actually, I suspect that a good three-quarters of those sexual harassment cases which cause such pious headshaking are due to nothing but poor psychotribology in the workplace. When a doctor accuses a partner of public fondling, or a woman erupts with fury at being consistently called 'sweetheart', it is not straightforward sex war. There can be antipathies stronger and less rational than any mere passion. Stray phrases betray it: 'She had an unfortunate manner' or 'He had always thought he was too good for the job.' Sex itself is a squeaky wheel: sometimes the very presence of a nubile woman workmate – whose Lycra bodysuit is, in fact, a statement about having lost 12 lb, not about sexual rapacity – can deeply infuriate men whose own love-lives are a bit ropy and who come to work partly in order to *stop* thinking about Lycra and pouting lips . . . If they harass her, it could be that her very presence is – tribologically speaking – harassing them first. It is no excuse, but it is an explanation.

And remember, just as you can be chivalrous and loving towards a direct rival with whom your gears mesh smoothly, so equally you can fall into a frenzy of hate about a quite innocent colleague. For all kinds of weird reasons: because she has a silly accent, because she always wears four-inch spike heels and a tight little skirt, because she keeps on agreeing with you and saying, 'Well, this is it.' Or because his shoes squeak *on purpose* (we are not in rational areas here); because he has a deep annoying masculine Freemason sort of laugh that makes you want to assault him with a crowbar; because he has pictures of three grinning kids on his desk and you are having an access battle over yours; because he doesn't drink. Add a habit of tunelessly humming *Abide with Me* under the breath, a hot summer's afternoon and a frustrating meeting with a client, and you have all the ingredients for a good Agatha Christie stabbing any day.

Except that violence rarely breaks out. The people concerned merely squeak and grind and grate against one another, sending acrid fumes of resentment across the office. Whenever Personnel tries to investigate, everyone says through gritted teeth, 'No – very good worker – can't complain.' It is the hate which dare not speak its name.

And what will the psychotribologist do? Why, lubricate them, of course. First with drink: I will take the grinding gears out separately for lunch and winkle out of them what tuneless hum, what particular way of laughing Nyah-nyah-nyah on the telephone, what deliberate inability to change the paper in the fax machine has brought on this helpless enmity. The next step is to move into that office myself for a week, and guarantee to be so annoying that everyone will unite in detesting me. I have a particularly good line in singing 'Ya picked a fine time to leave me, Lucille' under my breath, and my reminiscences of convent schooldays have brought deskmates to their knees in days. After I go, nothing will ever seem so bad again. I shall charge a great deal for this service.

10

Out of the girls' playground

I groan, I am disgruntled. The European Community has whopped out another report about women, of whom I seem to be one, detailing the excessive gruelling dreadful pressures we suffer in a male-dominated etcetera. So far, no complaint. I like a bit of a grumble. Working mothers face a 'major dilemma'. Still no complaint.

Then they go and wreck it all by finding that women want 'job satisfaction and human contact' while men want 'higher incomes and rapid promotion'. Hah! The same old story. Women want to be nurses, carers, devoted secretaries, teachers and cosy old bodies in Personnel. Men want to screech along the fast track regardless, their only human contacts resulting in a trail of corpses. Women want rubber-plants in the office, men want BMWs. Women like writing sensitive articles about what their child said when it found the hamster dead, and men want to get into battledress and gallop off a landing-craft with forty marines and a microphone. Or, at least, to test themselves to destruction out on the stump with Field-Marshal Ashdown. Women want love, and men want money. Pah!

That there is a grain of truth in the above is what makes it so very irritating. Any survey of callow teenage girls and boys reveals that the girls lean towards personal life and humane values, and the boys towards red Porsches. If there was a Mr World competition it is doubtful whether contestants would so readily lisp that they wanted to 'help people and work with children'. The female Robert Maxwell has not yet dawned over the red horizon. And at a certain point in life, it is undeniable that the fearful hormones of motherhood do slosh around and cause unprofessional thoughts such as: 'Poor old J.D., he looked like a lost little boy when I hit him with those figures, better back off.' Many is the Ms Macbeth who has cried under her breath 'Unsex me here!' as she tripped into the boardroom, and nonetheless found herself reaching out a helping hand to a young colleague with big troubled toddler eyes, who will later stab her in the back. Women had been sidling into the slow lane for their families' sake for years before Norman Fowler ever thought of it. There is truth in the truism, all right.

But it is not the whole truth. None of us is wholly masculine or feminine: I like Jan Morris's image of gender as a long, graduated scale on which the pointer of biological sex is set, almost randomly. Plenty of men look for human contact and moral satisfaction at work – how the hell else do we run the Health Service? And plenty of women wouldn't half mind a bit of fast promotion and serious money. Nor are we even talking about effete men and butch women: if you want to find Real Men working for peanuts because they love humanity, drop in at any Adventure Centre. You will find it full of enormous hunky beasts called Rob and Mick whose passion for abseiling is overshadowed by their passion for reclaiming lost and timid human souls and giving them some self-respect. And if you want to find a ruthless, venal, ambitious woman in any office, just listen out for the most tinkling female laugh and don't get under those four-inch heels.

Oh yes, women can do it, all right. Nastily. There is a new exhibition at the National Maritime Museum about pirates, including the eighteenth-century women Mary Read and Anne Bonny, and its curator admiringly says that they were 'every bit as bloodthirsty, bold and daring as any male pirate. They fought duels and were in the thick of the action.' They even swung the ultimate female trick by avoiding the hangman through well-timed pregnancies. Their spiritual great-granddaughters are still with us, still looting and pillaging in their ladylike way.

And never mind the variable dimension of sex: what about the dimension of time? Many of us start our careers as dewy-eyed idealists, become disillusioned and hastily cultivate hearts of stone, make our way ruthlessly upwards, then have a happy crisis of life and conscience and change back again. It is not only women who get overcome by motherhood and gentle yearnings: middle-aged men are surprisingly prone to sudden alterations of ambition. Ask Sir James Goldsmith, now busy saving the planet. Ask the tropical mining-engineer who grabbed early retirement and turned his back on zinc deals forever to retrain as a schoolteacher. Ask the legendary BBC correspondent who found God and horrified his employers by bursting in and demanding to give back all the expenses he had fiddled during his heathen years. Ask anyone who has been jolted – by a marriage, a death, an illness – into reviewing his life. Only don't then tell him that because he has hair on his chin, he must perforce care only for money and promotion. And don't tell women that all human kindness springs from the ovary. Such typecasting diminishes us all.

And, equally to the point, it stops some of us ever getting promoted.

11

This is the head that was hunted in vain . . .

A headhunter rang me the other week. There, I've said it. You were going to turn the page, weren't you? Suspecting insufferable vainglory and some turgid account of how they offered me the Midland-and-Shanghai Bank Chairmanship with five hundred K and a dress allowance – well, pleaded really – and how I told them heck, no, I couldn't desert my public.

And who is to say that I did not have some such fleeting thoughts myself? After all, a fresh eye, a woman's touch, the earthy savoir-faire of an experienced mother might be just what they thought they needed at the helm of today's caring multinational. Was Eurodisney in leadership trouble already? Or was Someone cautiously spreading the net a bit wider in the search for a Palace press officer? Or a woman High Court judge, rocky on law perhaps but qualified to deliver snappy 800-word judgements complete with matching headline?

Well, they weren't. Frankly, the job was part-time, ill-defined, governmental and clearly likely to prove so aggravating that they will be lucky to get Roland Rat. Nor did the time fit in, nor was the money great. Nor would I have been any good at it whatsoever. So amicably we drifted apart, Mr Headhunter and I.

Oh, but I did enjoy those low, murmurous conversations, those assurances of discretion, that assignation in a discreet corner of the Savoy foyer. I challenge anyone not to. A cynical headhunter once told me that almost everybody (except a few disappointingly down-to-earth women of a certain age) visibly preens at the first approach. What they most want to know is 'Who brought my name up?' It is like the moment when you get into that secretive institution, *Who's Who*, suddenly in mid-career and for no clear reason: you feel as if you had been singled out by grey, powerful, infinitely perceptive figures like those chaps in John Buchan novels who are always calling our hero in to Sir Walter Bullivant's office and saying things like: 'We've watched you, Hannay, ever since the business at Rooivaterstrand, and you seem to have the kind of nerve we need for a tricky job'. It's always nice to be watched and approved of. Ask any three-year-old.

It all came back to me during this week's rash of media speculation and articles by recruitment consultants about what use might be found for a slightly battered former leader of the Labour Party. Lucky, lucky Mr Kinnock! He will be getting the discreet phone calls now, the Savoy meetings, the unexpected suggestions. 'We realize you may never have considered this sort of work but we think – and our client thinks – that you have the qualities we're looking for.' And there he will be, off in a lovely daydream about becoming headmistress of Roedean, or Governor of the Falklands with plumes in his hat, or taking over from Phillip Schofield in *Joseph and the Amazing Technicolour Dreamcoat*. Schofield himself is a case in point: when the Really Useful Company rang him saying 'Can you sing?' he says he thought it would be 'some dodgy pantomime in Woking' and tried to put them off. When they made the Palladium offer, he thought it was a hoax then went into shock. A perfect headhunting scenario.

Except, of course, that Phillip Schofield actually took the job, was a clever choice, and does it rather well. The thrills I am talking about are the kind which wear off when you begin to contemplate the actual job. Some of us are incurable fantasists who read the appointments pages and Mitty ourselves into every role which does not boringly require paper qualifications. I have spent many a happy minute briefly taking on the role of 'Regional Arts Supervisorperson' or 'Go-ahead trainee reporter, Darlington Herald'. The words 'Applications are invited for . . .' have me flying happily from cloud to cloud, mentally sharpening new pencils and laying them out on an imaginary clear new desk. That I am not even sure what a Head of Supply does, or a

Compliance Advisor, or a Group Financial Director, does not stop me dreaming.

But the point of being headhunted is that it takes the process one step further. Someone else is daydreaming on your behalf. If you are naturally diffident about your own abilities and lack singleminded ambition, it is marvellous to have an authoritative, experienced, suave headhunter come up to you and say 'Barclays de Zoete Wedd has just the niche for you!' If you live in a ragged, unformed freelance way, unsure what you will do next time a particular employer gets sick of you, such bland self-assurance is a powerful drug. Condé Nast magazines once hypnotized me into editing the *Tatler* this way, sending down big BMWs to get me and the baby-basket in the snow and expansively refusing to listen when I explained that I disliked Society. It took six months to tunnel out. History did try to repeat itself three years later, but in the nick of time I stuffed my ears with cottonwool and tied myself to the mast, like Ulysses' sailors passing the sirens' rock. You have to when you're just a girl who cain't say no.

So I am slowly learning. And there is even a perverse thrill in being invited, and refusing. Ask Edwina Currie about that sometime.

12

Threadings

*S*ocial rituals are a serious matter. We could not do without chris- tenings and enthronements, inductions and coronations, launch- ings, swearings-in and passings-out, weddings and threadings. Do not omit this last: in our household the ceremonies known as 'Threadings' have taken on an awesome significance over the years. Televised, they cause marital discord because my husband can sit for hours watching them and shouting 'Oh, not her!', whereas I have to leave the room after ten minutes with hot flushes and crawling sensations on the skin.

A Threading is, of course, an awards ceremony. More precisely, an awards ceremony in which the main action consists of overwhelmed people in evening dress threading their way through dozens of tightly-packed dinner-tables to a podium, where they receive the Best Supporting Award and – in extreme cases – make a speech thanking director, aromatherapist and aged mother in Pontypridd. The TV convention is that during the actual threading process one camera mercilessly follows the man in the black tie or woman in ruffles, hoping that he or she will trip over a table-leg or get lost and blunder into the Gents. A second lens scans the audience to catch the near-miss rivals grimacing, shredding their napkin or laughing tinklingly to their companions to show they don't care.

The rot began with the Oscars and Emmys and Oliviers. But you can't blame actors: their lives are brutal and uncertain, and they need to cheer themselves up with a bit of tinselly threading. But then it spread to the Baftas, both performance and craft; to the Sonys for radio, and Bookers and Whitbreads for writers. It went beyond books to serve magazines (at least two major award ceremonies each year) and newspapers, which beat even Hollywood for sheer glutinous self-congratulation. Gradually more and more professions, even sciences, have plunged joyfully into the world of white napery and white-knuckle public suspense, of deadly slow openings of envelopes and that endless, remorseless zig-zagging between tables. Or, in my case, sliding beneath them overcome by formless emotion.

I never quite know why I feel like this. There is nothing really wrong with Threadings. This week I was at the Grosvenor House Hotel with hundreds of magazine editors, publishers and writers. It was OK: we gossiped, scanned shortlists by candlelight and clapped various Editors, Publishers and Writers of the Year. There was nothing to fear – unless you count the extremely noisy table next to us which erupted hysterically at every mention of *The Publican* magazine – and I cannot deny that as human activities go, it was harmless. No doubt at this very moment half a dozen professional gangs are cooking up virtually identical ceremonies to crown the Dental Hygienist of the Year or whatever. Why shouldn't they?

Still I tremble. I can't even plead that I was disillusioned by Baftagate or the sicko Oscars for *Silence of the Lambs*; nor even the fact that every judging panel I have ever sat on has ended up muttering, 'Oh God, chalk and cheese, how do you judge, might as well toss for it.' If a lack of total justice were enough to sink a ritual, we'd barely put up with the Queen's Speech. No, I have no rational case against awards ceremonies. Because of this I have tried to conform, serving over the years as a judge, nominator, prizegiver and speechmaker. I have even been shortlisted (mercifully, never had to thread, couldn't have done it, would rather die). But the dread still rises every time.

So I tried an experiment. Halfway through the magazine dinner, feeling unsettled as usual, I closed my eyes and emptied my mind in the hope of reliving and exorcising the trauma. It worked. In that moment of darkness I saw Reverend Mother, wrinkled as a holy tortoise, sitting on her chair with an expression of inscrutable menace. I saw rows of little girls in white blouses, hands folded, eyes forward. I saw the Mistress of Discipline tugging briefly at her wimple before beginning to read out the list of prizes. 'Fourth Class.

The prize for Merit goes to Lucinda Badleigh-Shaken. Next in Merit: Lavinia Barren-Knight.' Lucinda and Lavinia would rise and walk towards the Reverend Chair, before which lay a parterre of flowers brought in by a gnarled lay-sister. Each little girl then had to curtsey in front of the parterre, walk round it without taking her eyes off Reverend Mother, curtsey again, receive her book or certificate, then – pay attention, girls! – *walk backwards and sideways around the parterre* without kicking it. Then curtsey one more time and walk back through the silence to her seat, which might be three ranks back on a precarious structure of benches and steps. Only then would the next prize be announced. It took hours. And it stopped me ever again wanting to be given a prize in public.

I opened my eyes and I was back in the murky candlelight of Park Lane, mechanically applauding *Gardeners' World* magazine. Perhaps the daydream was therapeutic and the nightmare will now die. Thank you, doctor, for listening so patiently.

13

I used to be . . .

I was listening to the election of the new Speaker of the House of Commons, admittedly in a rather Eurovision spirit of irresponsibility, when I suddenly realized why I was backing Betty Boothroyd against Peter Brooke. Never mind her doughty years on the backbenches, never mind his Ulster record, never mind their comparative skills in chairmanship: I reluctantly faced the fact that I favoured Miss Boothroyd mainly because she used to be a Tiller Girl. And Mr Brooke used to be a management headhunter. No comparison really, is there?

Of course it is irrational. These things were long ago, and divided from the present-day Boothroyd and Brooke by many other achievements. We should not be romantic, I tell myself firmly. That bygone hoofer has little to do with today's politician. And yet somehow, the knowledge of someone's first – or very early – job throws an aura round them for life.

It is like hearing about a friend's first love: it turns him from a sound-bite into a whole novel. We feel at home with people when we know how they started. We like to think of John Major carrying hods, Alexei Sayle digging twelve days' worth of the Jubilee Line, and Madonna getting the push from the Dunkin' Donut for squirting jam at a customer. We are glad to hear about Aristotle Onassis in a steam laundry, Lord Snowdon as a motorbike dispatch-rider and Henry Kissinger's undistinguished career in a shaving-brush factory in New York. And Benny Hill, rest his soul, was a real milkman long before he wrote his song about 'Ernie, the fastest milkman in the West'. Gary Cooper was a milkman, too. So was Freddie Garritty of Freddie and the Dreamers who, when he heard that BBC Manchester was auditioning, 'rounded up the Dreamers and drove the milk float as fast as I could to Television Centre'. So that's what happened to the Gold Top.

For many of these I am indebted to Geoff Tibballs, compiler of a odd volume called *First Jobs of The Famous* (Sphere Books). Also to him goes credit for more widely disseminating the news that during his penurious years in Vienna Hitler designed advertising posters for a deodorant called *Teddy*. 'Ten thousand steps a day are a pleasure with Teddy Powder' was the slogan, with a drawing of a man wringing out his sock. You see what I mean? There's magic in such knowledge. Could anything else have made you warm, even momentarily, to Adolf Hitler, other than this proof that he was once a desperate hack like you and me (well, me anyway)?

Celebrities know this, and often milk their first jobs shamelessly for glamour and credit. For a long time no young British novelist dared publish without a jokey list of previous jobs to go with the photo on the back flap: 'Former shoe polish salesman, wine waiter and bookie's runner . . .' gave a raffish, man-of-the-world air to the most callow youth, even if the truth was that none of the jobs lasted more than a week before he settled in to the Rating and Valuation Office for fifteen years. Actors and politicians like to establish street credibility by mentioning early jobs in interviews: how else do we know that Norman Tebbit, Richard Burton and Tony Hancock all served as menswear salesmen? PR companies foisting guests on chat show researchers always give lists of picaresque previous jobs, and many is the author who has arrived in a local radio station to find the host mainly interested in his stint as a chicken-sexer. Sheepishly, the subject then admits that it was only for two days.

The more often this happens, the edgier he gets. I have watched many famous eyes narrow in pure hatred as I innocently read out their potted biography in a studio. I do not think that Maurice Micklewhite, a.k.a. Michael Caine, really wants to be told any more times that he used to be a Smithfield meat porter. I suspect Glenda Jackson is fed up with the Boots the Chemist story. But serve them right for telling anyone in the first place: they should know that first jobs are never forgotten. As with first loves, the reality may have been a pointless and unfruitful fumble, but the legend is everything.

And it is a two-edged sword. For every chief executive who courts popularity by boasting about his days as an office boy at 3/6d a week, there is someone else deliberately keeping things vague. Mrs Thatcher's industrial chemistry background sounded great until some nosy researcher reported that her speciality was working out how much air you could whip into soft ice-cream before it collapsed. Neither the circus nor the garden gnomes are any longer an asset to Mr Major. And once you are on the Booker shortlist, or indeed named Financial Journalist of the Year, it could be seriously annoying to know that the Oxbridge element among your rivals were able to mince around saying 'Well, she started out on *My Guy* magazine, old habits die hard, know what I mean?'

Such people should instantly invent a new provenance. Grave-digging is always very hip, I find. Especially if you haven't got the legs to convince anyone you were a Tiller Girl.

14

Fowler's Law

I know I am a figure of derision, pointed at like something in a
Pont cartoon. *'See that woman?* She's – har har – the journalist
who believed Norman Fowler really resigned to spend more time
with his family! *Talk about naïve!'* Modish opinion always had it that
what Sir Norman really wanted, two years ago, was to see less of
his Prime Minister. There was a curious jeering tone amongst male
commentators at the very idea that a chap might slow down his
career in order to be home for nursery tea with five-year-old Isobel
and eight-year-old Kate. It was as if Sir Bob Reid had announced
that he would have to give up restructuring BR because his hamster
was poorly.

Now, of course, the jeerers are preening themselves on having
been right all along. This, they say, is proved by the fact that Sir
Norman has edged back into the fast lane as Party chairman. 'Seen
enough of his family, has he?' they crow. 'Hah!'

But I hold the faith. It is perfectly possible – in fact, come to think
of it, inevitable – that Sir Norman's family has changed in two years.
Grown up a bit. You know, chaps: that thing which children tend
to do while you are in Frankfurt. If the youngest is now seven, the
odds are she eats her tea a bit later. Goes to Brownies, maybe.
Plays computer games round at her friends' house. She will have
developed a powerful enough intellect to realize that Daddy still
loves her even when he is out cracking the Party whip. There is
a big difference between five and seven years old, just as there is
a vast gulf between three and five. As one fast lane Daddy told

me: 'Once they're eight, they think it's rather a laugh when you send them faxes from Bangkok and bring back gold hats. When my daughter was four I used to let my colleagues do all the good travelling, because she cried every time I got the suitcase down.' Family life, as that man knew, is never quite the same game two years running.

Herein lies a profound truth: and if we would only grasp it, a comforting one too. Somehow a legend has grown up that you can only be one of two things. You can, says the cliché, be a whizzy professional who wrenches herself from the cradle after four weeks, never gets home till nine and embraces the dreary concept of 'weekend quality time'. Or you can stay home for ten years glueing eggboxes together and making damson jam in pinafored penury. If you are a man, you either 'take your career seriously' or be a henpecked house-wimp forever.

Hokum. Unless you deliberately have a large number of widely spaced children, the years of utter 24-hour dependency are brief. Certainly compared to a lifetime's career. Suppose you are a woman in a good job: you might work until you were twenty-eight, have a baby, come back for a year to get away from the nappies, have another baby a year later, mislay your nanny and decide to give up work during the complicated years of double toddler-management, later start part-timing to fit in with nursery school and an au pair's language lessons – perhaps with a bit of help from a husband marking time in the slow lane and bringing work home – then advance to a full day once the children are at school. With, of course, the caveat that you refuse to go to six o'clock bonding sessions down at the pub or work late for no good reason. You are confident because you never stopped for long, you are relaxed because you have not done yourself or your family any emotional violence; and for heaven's sake, you are still only thirty-four.

And by the time you are forty ('Sleek, chic and at your peak' as a recent book unkindly told us to be) you have a pair of sassy sub-teens who know you well, have had plenty of time with you, and are quite prepared to put up with your rapidly accelerating career in return for ski holidays and not having to eat your home-made jam.

Even those who start families later can pause, tread water and start again, provided that they are cunning and pragmatic about it (and you get a hell of a lot more cunning after forty). When to scale down the work or sideline it is up to you: some children are perfectly happy with a nanny while they are toddlers, but later become desperate for parents to be at the school gate in person several times a week. Others cling to your legs and follow you to the lavatory for five years, and then discard you utterly in favour of their schoolfriends. So you take your break or skip your promotion when common sense and loving kindness (and economic realism) tell you that the time has come. And it is not the end of your career. Suppose you were ill for a year or two, or kidnapped by Lebanese guerrillas, or even banged up for insider trading, you wouldn't write yourself off, would you? Well, then. Go with the flow.

All right, of course it isn't easy. Nothing worth doing ever is. There are days when you wish one or the other of your duties would just go away. But that's real life: and if Sir Norman Fowler has had a go at it, good for him.

Not least because his name is now first-rate ammo for wives to throw at thrusting husbands who insist that getting home for the school play would spell permanent professional disaster.

15

April blues

*I*t begins at school, when you sit by the window in double Maths
and someone is mowing the playing-field and a waft of warm
intoxicating grassy air comes in on the breeze. And you look out
and say, echoing Mole of *Wind in the Willows*: 'Oh bother, oh drat,
oh blow. Hang spring-cleaning! Damn Pythagoras!' It carries on
through university, where a sadistic system decrees that the balmy
days of youthful summer should be spent in musty libraries reading
John Stuart Mill while the river of life flows past outside. It was at
that point in my life that I wrote a lousy little poem which I have
never been able to get out of my head: so tauntingly, jinglingly,
does it ring. It began:

> I woke one April morning
> To the merry cuckoo's shout
> And went into the library
> For spring had left me out.
> The flowers bloomed, the birdies sang,
> Fresh sprang the fresh spring onion
> But I was in the library
> Evaluating Bunyan . . .

It had a Miltonic 'aery spirit' in it later, I remember, who sang
'Oh see the little newborn calf against its mother's flanks!/It'll make
a lovely binding for my book on German banks . . .'

Every year since, spring has left me out again. The first rays of warm
lifegiving sun have found me underground in the Ryvita-panelled,

dead airlessness of studios with a whey-white face and a knotted neck. Or hunched at a keyboard, staring out through plate glass at the Directors' car park. Sometimes, which is almost worse, my resentful stare has been through a study window at home, out on to the green lawn, where a nanny romped carefree with my brown babies. It is vile, unnatural. It makes you want to fling off all your clothes, raise two fingers to responsibility and skip off in tattered jeans to join a hippy convoy. Or the Duchess of York, according to your taste in company.

But it is where most of us are, is it not? We may be off today, but tomorrow we shall be back in our rightful hateful place: most of us urban workers, pallid, slug-like, loathsome indoor creatures, with the cruel sun making a mockery of our annually increasing wrinkles. Another spring, another step towards the grave, and oh woe! we are shut in smelly cities and smellier trains, where even sunshine is a pollutant as it raises acrid oily gases off the very tarmac. And every night, Michael Fish comfortingly pops up to tell us that the air quality today is 'poor'.

When the sun strikes in on the grimy photocopier and makes a mockery of the neon ceiling lights, urban workers feel bitterly alienated. We long for winter to come again so that we can wrap the office round us like a comforting fuggy old rug, and forget what a miserable prison it is. Come April, May, and especially glorious June, we don't want to bang keyboards or trade Eurobonds or serve in shops. Not us! Not with the blood warming up in our veins! We want to go out and roll around in long green grass, romp through meadows, run into the sea. In enlightened schools they sometimes greet the first fine weather of the year with 'Right, no lessons, everybody outside!', believing in the poet Martial's dictum that healthy children don't need to learn anything academic in the summer months. This belief, alas, has not caught on in offices. The best you get is the mingy annual holiday and fifty minutes in the park at lunchtime eating diet sandwiches and breathing in fumes. The whole thing is made worse by the unpredictability of English weather: agonized outdoor types stare gloomily out of their offices in early summer sunshine knowing perfectly well that this might turn out to be all there is for the year, and that they are missing it.

It is just as well they asked me to start this column in the chill days of February. My work-ethic, usually strong, starts to melt at this time of year. If it had been a warm spring day when I was asked for the first time to contemplate the labyrinth of working life, I would probably have scrawled POOH, I HATE WORK, HOORAY FOR THE HOLS in very large writing and left it at that. Curiously, later in the summer it would be all right: by August when everything wilts and shrivels I am generally in a pencil-sharpening, back-to-school mood. It is just spring that torments me so.

Fortunately, I now have proof that I am not alone in this feeling, and can therefore present my feelings as a newsworthy universal truth. A while ago I asked a few acquaintances in various business worlds to look over their colleagues' shoulders while they were in meetings and on the phone, to see if the doodles on the notepad changed with the seasons. It is a very small survey, but significant. I can reveal from one bank, one medical practice and a local authority that, at a very senior level, this past week men in particular have been drawing desert islands and palm trees. And boats. And women in swimsuits (the sexist beasts, how could they?). A month ago, my informants say, these same chaps were doodling the usual cars and houses and brick walls which indicate that their minds are well-and-truly geared into the ratrace of earning money and paying for sensible things.

So if you are thinking of offering anybody voluntary redundancy, early retirement or a posting to somewhere without much prestige but with somewhere to tie their boat up, take a tip from me. Do it in May. The victim will leap at it.

16

Mario land

I see that more schoolteachers have raised the alarm about children who get addicted to computer games (the offspring, it would seem, of parents suffering from such inferiority complexes about computers that they can't bring themselves to switch the damn things off by force). Having recently become hosts to SuperMario, his thick brother Luigi and a number of two-dimensional Japanese Kamikaze turtles, we can vaguely sympathize.

But only vaguely. Much more pressing is the growing addiction of a pair of working parents to sneaky lunch-hour sessions, late-night brooding battles with Bowser the Dragon and an alarming Mario Identification Syndrome. It is only one game which does this to us: we are left cold by the war games and tedious football simulations which the children intermittently borrow off friends. But Mario, poor little graphic in his flat hat, has won our hearts. He is not a fighter, whatever the instructions pretend. What he is having is a career, and it reminds us painfully of our own.

Let me tell you about Mario. He sets out across the screen as we all do, terribly small in stature and unarmed against the world. He is menaced by owls and ducks who want to throw him off the wall (the booklet says they are mushrooms and turtles, but we can't see it). You have to jump on the owls to kill them. But when you jump on the turtle-ducks, they go into their shells and then nip out again when you aren't looking, and push you off the wall.

As in anyone's early career, the knack is to jump up and down a lot and bang your head on a brick wall until you get some money out of it. Bang the right brick and a magic mushroom blooms and rolls off. If you can catch the mushroom you grow three times as big and become eligible for weapons, such as a fire-flower which enables you to zap owls at a distance, or a racoon suit which means you can fly, rather half-heartedly and for short distances, by swishing your tail.

On you run, swishing and killing assorted wildlife and getting on to exciting new levels of management at which you leap from tree to tree, swim amongst hostile jellyfish or creep through a claustrophobic, low-ceilinged, windowless castle ruled by a nasty spitting old dragon. To defeat him you sneak round behind him on a shaky platform, get an axe and cut the bridge from under his feet so he sinks without trace. To do this it helps to have amassed extra lives, which you do by collecting all the money in sight. The children shriek 'Dad! Get more money! Otherwise you'll never make it to the highest levels!' You see what I mean? This is not some infant fairytale. This is about business life. Robert Maxwell probably played it. Well.

But the really chilling thing is what happens to Mario when he is swaggering along, walking tall with his fire-flower on his hip, and he falls foul of an unexpected duck or fireproof beetle. Or if he fails to sneak round behind the Maxwell dragon, or puts his trust on a flying platform which sinks beneath him. He shimmers horribly, and *shrinks*. Right back to the diminutive, unarmed, trainee status he began with. The children call it 'being smalled', and think no more of it: for adults, it brings on a flood of instant recall of our worst days ever. Sometimes it only takes a word, or a memo, or a choicely phrased letter of scorn from a reader, or a bad moment at the staff party, and we are smalled. So we bleed for Mario. Once he is little and demoralized it only takes one passing owl to knock him right off the screen into early retirement. All that can save him is having amassed the money to buy into a new life. Or occasionally, having the sheer resilience and chutzpah to keep head-butting brick walls until a new mushroom renews his status.

I think it was Orwell who said that, viewed from within, every life is a succession of small defeats. The Japanese invented this game and they know a thing or two about losing face. So picture us, a pair of poor hacks, veterans of many a small defeat, sitting over a cup of cold coffee on a bad day trying to nurse valiant little Mario through his journey. Sometimes we get to level four, firing away and feeling bullish, then miss our stroke and shimmer back into nonentity. Then we leap despairingly at a brick, and out comes the mushroom of opportunity and we jump to grab it – and, too late, notice the ravine at our feet. Sometimes we catch the mushroom, grow big, and still fall down the hole. Never having amassed enough money we are written off, and the screen flashes GAME OVER.

At which point the children come in and demand their toy back, pouring scorn meanwhile on our low score, failure to get into World Seven, dearth of money and ignorance of the fact that there was a magic leaf all the time which would have turned us into flying racoons. They go ahead and demonstrate.

But they are young and heartbreakingly optimistic. They do not know how our hands grow unsteady on the buttons as we empathize with poor Mario, out there in the harsh working world which we know and they do not. All we can do is admire their technique, and wish them many magic mushrooms in the future.

17

Follow the van

See them walk: in a long, disconsolate file they go, eastward from bright Whitehall towards the grim dockland towers of Ozymandias Wharf. 'So many,' as T. S. Eliot would say, 'I had not known death had undone so many . . .' It would seem, in other words, that the 4,000 civil servants earmarked for the Canary Wharf experience are not entirely content with their lot. Barry Ramsbottom, General Secretary of their union, rather churlishly observed: 'We don't see why we should be dragged down the river to satisfy a private sector bungle.'

To an outsider, it seems reasonable for the Civil Service to save us money and use up otherwise pointless office space. But Mr Ramsbottom's words will strike a deep chord in many, because this has been a nomadic decade for office workers. We had the eighties boom with its mergers and takeovers and launches and regroupings; and now the nineties recession bringing collapses and rescues and yet more takeovers. All these things, whether fundamentally good or bad for business, always seem to entail hundreds of poor devils in office moves. No longer do companies engrave their names in stonework on the front, for their premises are just another asset and they may not be there long.

Merry-go-round relocation has become epidemic: all over the capital city Swiss-cheese plants are dying of environmental confusion, and in the second-hand office equipment shops of the Old Kent Road there are kneehole desks which have been into liquidation half-a-dozen times. I was looking one over, and found a drawer still full of clients' letters. A friend of mine found a hard disc in a filing cabinet, idly plugged it in to his computer and got an extremely useful mailing list. Someone may be missing thes things.

One company I deal with has had five different offices since 1982, having been independent, merged, then assimilated and spat out by no fewer than three large corporate owners. Small publishing companies in particular are victims, with staff often pathetically ringing up writers to say, 'We seem to have moved, we're in this tower thing in Croydon, all happened a bit suddenly, could you send another copy of the typescript down here?' Sometimes they feel so precarious they never even unpack the cardboard boxes, and so demoralized they can't be bothered to tack up the photographs of the staff party with rude speech-bubbles on, or the witty sign saying DON'T ASK ME I ONLY WORK HERE. Since work, and journeys to work, are part of daily individual life, the personal effect can be immense: as for the business effect, it would be interesting to have someone cost out on a national scale the expense of repeated office moves in terms of lost time, lost files, friction, and lateness of staff who took the wrong bus.

But perhaps you get used to it in the end, and develop a proud nomadic culture, pitching your computers like Bedouin and enjoying the ever-changing view (and ever-changing excuse not to send out cheques on time). Perhaps – hence the fear and loathing of the civil servants – it is the first move which is the worst: the one which uproots you from tradition. Moving out of a cosy familiar old building makes people nervous and chippy and critical and rootless. It is astonishing to observe how people who have worked quite happily in disgusting, cobwebby, inconvenient and frankly smelly surroundings for years will complain about trifles when transported to clean modern surroundings with state-of-the-art intelligent lighting and psychologically approved seating arrangements. It is the slum clearance programme all over again.

I speak with feeling, since for a period it looked as if Broadcasting House, that battleship-shaped building on Portland Place, my intermittent base for twenty years, was going to banish the departments where I work two days a week to the White City. It was not only the inconvenience (certain people openly admit to choosing a career in radio largely because it is so handy for John Lewis). It was love of the building itself. Not only does Reith's wraith still walk the corridors, scowling at the management's periodic attempts to jazz them up with new paintwork, but the place itself is as comfortable as a very old dressing-gown. Years ago on Long Beach, California, I toured that other 1930s monument, the *Queen Mary*, and felt strangely at home among the Bakelite and art deco. It took me half an hour to work out why.

We would have hated to lose those curving corridors, that strange smell of soup and armpits, mould and electronics; those glimpses through doors marked DANGER of Heath-Robinson pipework and yawning shafts to nowhere. Inconceivable to go to work without passing under the awful Eric Gill sculpture of Prospero and Ariel (off whose naked male member the artist was ordered to lop an inch or two for the sake of *pudeur*). With the rest of the battleship's crew, even I the part-timer quailed in fear.

We got our reprieve, and sail on safely for now. But spare a thought for those others, in other buildings, who by the storms of the restless modern age have been flung overboard lock, stock and rubberplant. Spare a thought for the reluctant new Canaries.

18

Money talks

There are some conversations you just don't hear in Britain. Like, 'What do you do?' Oh, consultant neurologist, eh? Money good, is it?' Or 'I did like your *Hamlet*, Mr Branagh. Nice income in Shakespeare, isn't there?' Nor 'What I love about being Archbishop/Admiral of the Fleet/Warden of All Souls is that they do pay bang on the nail!' The rule is that the higher you get up the tree the less you like the money to be mentioned. White collar types, creative souls, even field-marshals of industry tend to prefer the vocabulary of vocation and challenge and service.

Hence the expressions of pained surprise when shareholders or the media start to fuss about a chief executive's extra hundred thousand a year. 'The money is hardly relevant,' says the target plaintively from his Home Counties bunker. 'It's a question of competitiveness with the private sector . . . really a very small proportion . . . benefit to the company of attracting top talent . . .' And we media types have got a real brass neck anyway, complaining. The next Newsnight interviewer to raise an ironic, gentlemanly eyebrow at some highly-paid public servant should first don a large medallion with his own earnings (including after-dinner speaking) boldly written on it. Print journalists could just append the information to their byline, as in 'COME OFF IT, SIR RUPERT! Why should decent folk struggle while you take twenty per cent! says Glenda (half a million plus car) Slagg, Woman of the People.'

The Americans don't understand it, for this is a peculiarly British blend of hypocrisy and idealism. The more, and more secure, our salary the less we want to discuss it. We sail along, vocation and ideals of service gleaming like the proud upperworks of a ship, disguising what actually keeps us afloat.

Until, that is, someone rocks the boat, revealing its slimy, rusty, barnacled underside for a moment. Albert Finney gave it a lovely shove recently when he left a West End play because he hadn't been paid. Speaking on Michael Parkinson's radio show, Mr Finney is reported to have said, 'I discover that I have not been paid for some time and have decided to withdraw my services. If I'm not paid, I don't appear.' Imagine, my dears, the *frisson* in the upper reaches of theatre. Instead of talking exclusively about challenge and interpretation and how fabulous it is working with dear, dear Kate again, here we have a distinguished thesp coming on like a jobbing brickie. No pay, no play.

Myself, I find it oddly comforting. Just as it is comforting to quote Dr Johnson's 'Nobody but a blockhead ever wrote except for money.' I flung that one at a local writers' group once, in exasperation at their having invited me round in order to tell me that anyone published commercially was guilty of selling out and compromising with the media barons. The correct attitude for a writer was to be full of integrity, independent of public taste, and unread by any but the fellow-cognoscenti of the circle. There was a lot of this uppitiness around after the sixties, magically linking old money and Young Socialism. The feeling is rarer now, except among the kind of artists who do pretty well anyway out of Channel 4.

But vicious and unfair as it may sometimes be, there is something healthy about the marketplace. A labourer is worthy of his hire, and if that is not recognized everything goes sour. Witness the long conspiracy to describe nurses as angels and policemen as saints while paying them peanuts. It is nice to have a Finney occasionally, to make the link robustly on behalf of all. He might even give me, the world's weakest character in these matters, courage to tell a particular magazine that despite our agreeable meetings of minds on the telephone, I'm not sending in the next piece until they stump up for last April's, so there.

Yet the idealism fights back. That piece means something to me. I want to send it. Who wants to be a mere mercenary? In every field there are ideals of service: men who turn out late on Christmas Eve to mend your boiler and charge not a penny extra, doctors who spend private time on NHS patients out of interest and kindness, big-name actors who work for £160 a week because the play is the thing.

Perhaps the knack is for both parties to admit the situation openly. Charles Handy, the management writer, advocates making a distinction between paid work and gift work: as long as you know which you are doing at any given moment, you don't mind. Finney's 'I discover that . . .' is significant. Maybe if that play's management had called the cast together and said 'times are bad, the money's run out, but aren't we all having fun? Shall we try another week, do you think?' who knows what would have been the outcome? Maybe our silence about money is, in the end, an enemy of promise.

19

Whistleblowers

*W*e have been hearing a lot recently about those inconvenient employees who, in the familiar phrase, blow the whistle. The trigger was Robert Maxwell, followed by the GCHQ surveillance allegations; the issue was widened by the revelation of how hard it is to uncover NHS abuses if you have signed a gagging clause, and a riveting radio phone-in which stirred up the shrill, whistle-blowing ghosts of Mordecai Vanunu, Sarah Tisdall, Clive Ponting and a host of other martyrs to the cause of openness.

Every case stands on its own merits. But on a purely human level, if you have ever worked inside a tight organization it is difficult not to admire people who defy its grip and tell the world that the chemical plant is leaking, the power station making bombs, the government lying or the Matron of the old people's home modelling herself on Charles Laughton as Cap'n Bligh. They may only cross the road to the phone or the fax, or the road to a quiet cafe, but those few short steps would be too long a walk for most of us. Whistleblowers have to be dogged and principled, often loners, cussedly sure of their ground and angry enough to risk anything up to and including prison. And almost worse, they have to step outside the tribe. Even if you hate the tribe, that takes effort. Apart from the 'culture of disdain' eloquently described by Maxwell's biographer Tom Bower, there is a real struggle between professional ethics (sometimes not really all that ethical at all) and individual vision. Philosophers have argued for centuries over 'the greater good': whistleblowers put it into practice.

Idealistic disloyalty can happen on any scale. There was once a small-town articled clerk, fresh out of law school and keen as mustard, who couldn't help noticing that his principal's firm was abetting a grave injustice to a dead man's elderly, long-term cohabitee. The matter had a simple legal remedy under a new Act: a remedy about which the clerk knew, but which the old woman's lawyer had clearly forgotten. His decision was not easy. But small towns have pubs where legal opponents may drink, and where the names of recent Acts may be jotted on beermats. I believe the old woman got her money. Enough said.

But, as Sherlock Holmes would say, consider the curious incident of the dog in the night-time. 'The dog' protests Dr Watson 'did nothing in the night-time!' 'That' says Holmes smugly, 'was the curious incident.' For every insider who spots an evil and barks about it, there are dozens who lie doggo. Investigations into everything from the pindown of children to the pinching of pensions always seem to find other employees who saw everything and are – at last – eager to talk. Why not before?

At best, perhaps, it is a form of modesty. We might be wrong, we might not have the whole picture, better not interfere. Then again, it might be insensibility: a colleague of one civil servant who exposed a governmental economy-with-the-truth once told me that she worked in the same office as the mole, saw the same documents, but never thought to associate them with the opposite statements appearing in the newspapers at the time. 'Work is another world,' she said. 'You don't make the connections.' I believed her. But then, I am the only local reporter ever to have sailed past a burning garage on my moped and on seeing the four fire-engines outside, merely thought, 'Gosh, I suppose they have to fill up with diesel somewhere.' When I arrived to read the news bulletin which led on the garage fire, I realized that the peak of my crash-helmet must have obscured the smoke.

Then, of course, there is fear. All very well for outsiders to sneer at Maxwell's henchmen, but I once spent an hour in a small room with the big man and believe me, he was terrifying. Psychically terrifying: his gigantic ego left no room for anyone else's will. I can see that if you worked close enough to Maxwell to spot what he was doing, you might find out that when you tried to blow the whistle you just gasped, and swallowed the pea.

But the best answer to the question of the dogs who do not bark comes in a curious 1945 novel by C. S. Lewis, *That Hideous Strength*. I re-read it the other night, with a start of recognition. Largely an exercise in paranoia about godless scientists, the story features a Research Institute taking over the country and bulldozing market towns to build new vivisection labs. But there is a vivid moment when Mark Studdock, the youngest recruit and unsure of his acceptance by the inner ring of the Institute, walks into the library to find them all laughing by the fire. They have a job for him, his first definitely criminal act. Somehow Lewis, a veteran of Oxford college politics, knew all about such moments:

> There was no struggle, no sense of turning a corner. There may have been a time in the world's history when such moments fully revealed their gravity, with witches prophesying on a blasted heath or visible Rubicons to be crossed. But, for him, it all slipped past in a chatter of laughter, of that intimate laughter between fellow professionals which of all earthly powers is strongest to make men do very bad things before they are yet, individually, very bad men.

Packs a punch, does it not? Raises an echo? Well, it did with me. If not with you, good luck. May you never swallow the pea from your whistle.

20

Forty hours' hard

*T*here was something in the reporting of Mrs Gillian Shephard's hard-won EC concession over working hours which reminded me irresistibly of other negotiations, long ago. The Minister herself was circumspect in explaining her triumph, but her press allies cried 'Victory!' and 'a major triumph over the Euro lawmakers!' Then there were mutterings from the Institute of Directors about it not being such a good deal after all, thin end of the wedge, won at a high price, etc.

What it all reminded me of was school: small knots of triumphant fourteen-year-olds returning from the headmistress's study with their victories. 'We can walk into Tunbridge Wells in twos, not threes, *and* we persuaded her that we don't have to wear school hats because of Louella's allergy, *and* we've got permission to watch *The Man from Uncle*', they would crow, and the rest of us would try to pick holes in it by proving that they had only won these valuable concessions at some dreadful price like agreeing to wear 40-denier tights with seams. Who says education is not a full preparation for life? Clearly in the years to come there will be many a stimulating session of arguing ourselves out of compulsory Eurothings, and Britain will need me and Louella. Oh yes.

But the whole subject was wonderful saloon-bar stuff. Well, how many hours a week do *you* work? Do you get a minimum 11 hours rest ('Hah! Rest!' cry the working mothers, in chorus) between shifts, and 35-hour uninterrupted weekends? Do you want them?

See, everyone has an opinion, and nobody much agrees. A perfect Eurosubject.

For a start, think about 48 hours, the minimum which Britain was afraid of being bound to. It represents 9 to 5, six days a week. Or perhaps 8 to 6 every weekday, with a 4 o'clock finish on Fridays. It gets nowhere near a City workaholic's 7.30 am to 9 pm, nor to the life of a publican within the new extended hours or a mothers' help expected to be available for babysitting at night (nannies, unless they are careful, can run through 48 hours by Wednesday lunchtime). On the other hand, since we have now agreed to maximum eight-hour night shifts, anyone aiming at a 48-hour week would have to do six nights on the trot, plus travel. Not much of a life, really. Whereas the City chap above, and perhaps even the publican, might say their lives were fine.

Which is, in the end, why working hours are always going to be impervious to regulation. If contracts were only clear, and jobs plentiful enough to permit escape, we would probably all throw in the Eurosponge and reject any regulation at all. Because lives evolve and priorities shift, and what is outrageously inhumane for a struggling parent might be just perfect for a keen 22-year-old still enjoying that early love affair with learning a trade. Or for a singleminded careerist who rejoices in rapidly expanding responsibility and has no hobbies and few friends. Or, indeed, for a tigerish post-menopausal woman hurling herself back into the workplace with terrifying Thatcheresque zest.

I am happy to report that the EC recommendations make most of my past life retrospectively illegal. At school, if you count compulsory white-veil processions and hockey practice as work (and I most certainly did), I worked a clear 56-hour week. As a junior studio manager at Bush House I worked ten-hour night shifts, often involving harassment (well, bum-pinching) from the Latin American Section, bless them. On local radio I became so passionately enamoured of the medium that I worked seven days a week because the weekend was the only time they would let me stand around in damp fields with a microphone saying, 'Well, here I am at the site of today's re-enactment of the battle of Marston Moor, and here is Sid Anorak from the Sealed Knot, complete with genuine leathern ale-mug, to tell us all about it. Sid, what's that exactly that you've got on your head?' Well, no, I wouldn't do it now if I could help it: but at that age I didn't want my statutory 35-hour weekly rest period because all I would have done was mooch around waiting for Monday. When they did clamp down on the hours I ended up so desperate I joined a badminton club, over which we shall draw a veil. As Miss Austen says, let other pens dwell on guilt and misery; nor would I poach upon Mr Diamond and Ms Truss. Work alone kept me out of mischief in the single life.

But the most bizarre shifts of all occurred in an experimental period in the early 1970s when producers on the Radio 4 Today programme worked – wait for it – a week consisting of two 22-hour shifts. You started on, say, Monday at noon, and worked clear through to ten the next morning. Then you went to bed for a day or so, and came back on Thursday at noon to do the same trick. Officially you could go and lie down on a BBC bed for a while in the small hours, but if America or the Far East was busy, you didn't. And anyway, sometimes on the way to your bed-hour you fell into bad company and played a hand of poker with the commissionaires.

This had the advantage that there were no unwieldy handover sessions from day to night shift, with consequent losing of tapes and passing of bucks. It also quite suited both rootless trainees like me, and foxy old stagers who were combining the job with running a farm or a secret PR agency or several wifelets. It had the disadvantage that after a bit, everyone went rather odd.

They had to give it up in the end. But I am not sorry to have done it. What is life about, if not trying all sorts of weird ways in which to lead it? I think Louella and I will have to go into Europe and sort their ideas out a bit.

21

Class of '92

They will be leaving school soon for the last time, if they haven't already: the Class of '92, on the way to the rest of their lives. By and large it will be an undramatic rite of passage, because the British way of leaving is to shamble out, half-raising one hand in apologetic farewell. There will not even be a visible exodus, because at least half the nation's schoolforce will leave in dribs and drabs when their last exam is finished. As they mutter 'See-ya' to friends and occasionally teachers, they will be weeks away from even knowing whether they have got any qualifications. So no trumpets will sound, no flags flutter, to mark their passage into the working world.

I took this as being quite the normal way of things, unworthy of remark, until a few weeks ago I found myself in the Spa Pavilion at Felixstowe, sitting in the corner of a platform with Elgar's *Pomp and Circumstance* blaring out overhead. Before us, up silent aisles between a reverent audience, forty-five teenagers in academic gowns and mortarboards did an immaculate swaying slow-march towards the tiers of seats which dominated the centre stage, facing outwards. Then up rose a well-brushed girl signalled as 'Salutatorian' and an equally decorous 'Valedictorian', to make formal speeches on behalf of the Class of '92. Then someone sang 'My Wish for You' to the Class, and the Class sang back its Senior Song, and diplomas and scholarships were announced and someone said, 'The path of wisdom is like the first gleam of dawn, gleaming ever brighter towards morning,' and someone else quoted *The Hobbit* about how the road goes ever on. And the invited speaker (me) shuffled her

76

notes rapidly, cut most of the subversive flippant stuff out of the speech and tried to think of something inspiring enough to match the occasion.

You are there before me. Yes, indeed, it was no British school which laid on this jamboree. We have a USAF base here – for one year longer – and this was the penultimate Woodbridge American High School graduation ceremony. And I tell you, Colonel, I was pretty damn choked with pride to be there. Yessir, I was.

And I do not mock. I might have, at the first shock of formality. I am a child of the informalizing years, the decades which began with the shambling sixties. I have grown up into a world in which it is OK to express the view that suits are fascist, and where a British seventeen-year-old forced to do a slow-march and wear a mortarboard might well consider phoning Childline and having its tormentor carted off on a charge of ritual abuse. But ten minutes into this ceremony of exiled Americans, I was hooked.

I think it was the moment when the Principal stood in one corner of the stage with a tableful of diplomas, and senior teacher Carl Grover thundered out each name in turn, in full. 'Carl J. Muelchi!' he would yell, with palpable pride, or 'Corby J. Priddy!' – and some incongruously well-dressed crewcut would walk across the stage, alone, to deafening applause. Each student got a diploma (for all the marking is done by now, and those who fail don't get on stage at all) but the Principal handed them also a single flower. Or it might have been the final moment when Mr Grover said, 'Ladies and Gentlemen – The Class of '92!' and we all clapped and they all beamed and, with ineffable ceremony, each took the tassel from one side of their mortarboard and laid it down the other side to signal the moment of graduation. Then the kids descended from the dais, picked up waiting bouquets and ran down to give them to Mom and Dad. Gulp. Yes, Gulp. I could hardly see straight, even when the graduates had emerged on to the bleak Felixstowe seafront to hurl their mortarboards in the air and revert to the normal savage eighteen-year-old state.

School matters. It is the first workplace, the first wider tribe we belong to. Maybe we are wrong to let the children slouch away without ceremony other than the routine lacklustre prizegiving, without being celebrated as a graduating group, without even knowing their worth until the dread brown envelope arrives in mid-holiday. Mr Grover was no naïve optimist about the future of some of his Class of '92: yet the send-off they got conveyed a different message. It suggested they had come some way along the path of wisdom already, and that everyone was proud of them.

But perhaps British schoolteachers prefer to give more informal inspiration and advice to their charges at the moment of departure? I conducted a small survey of last words offered by friends' headteachers (and would, naturally, welcome more examples).

At a Northern grammar, my husband's headmaster spoke only once to his Sixth Form, to instruct them to read Virginia Woolf's *To the Lighthouse*, because it contained everything a young man needed to know. At my French convent, we small ones once heard the Reverend Mother exhorting the leavers in a thrilling whisper: 'One thing, *mes petits*. In your life, remember this. *Ne lisez jamais dans votre lit!*' Just why reading in bed should lead to depravity we never dared to ask. Girls' schools seem to specialize in mysterious diktats. 'Never let a boy touch your jersey' was a favourite in the sixties. And 'Only shopgirls eat in the streets.' But possibly the ultimate social and career advice was offered to young Etonians: 'Two things. *Don't* carry pens in your top pocket. And if a girl doesn't want to go swimming, don't make her.' And out they went, to rule the nation.

Give me the Spa Pavilion and a song from *The Hobbit* any day.

22

Après Tina, le deluge

*L*ast week's gasp-hot news was that Tina Brown, the glossy British editor who stormed New York society as editor of *Vanity Fair*, is to burrow even deeper into the heart of intellectual America as editor of the *New Yorker*. Good luck to her. My main identification with the story, I have to say, is with the chap called Graydon Carter who steps into her shoes at the magazine she picked up and sprinkled with her particular glitzy brand of fairy-dust eight years ago. When one paper rang him up he was more than ready to express his feelings.

'Tina', he said with graceful gallantry, 'has small feet which leave large tracks. They will be difficult to fill.' Say what you like about New York editors, they're quick on the draw with an epigram. You don't get that kind of stuff when one Bob Reid takes over from another at British Rail. Nor did Mr Major once remember to compliment Mrs Thatcher on the smallness of her feet.

But I feel for Mr Carter because I too, reader, have trodden those tracks. I followed Tina Brown at the last magazine she revived, the *Tatler*, and I can tell him what to expect. Ms Brown herself is no problem: she gives a brisk and generous handover before vanishing from sight, invariably upwards. But once she is gone, it is exactly like being the nameless, terrified, mousy heroine of Daphne du Maurier's *Rebecca*, with the part of the loyal yet sinister housekeeper Mrs Danvers played by a massed chorus of staff.

For nearly all her subordinates adored her. Several, indeed, found life so arid in the succeeding years that they emigrated to New York just to work for her again. But they displayed what I have since seen in other people who have worked for clever, charming, ambitious and emotionally tough bosses: a kind of quavering, half-worshipping half-resentful intensity. There was a palpable need to let the incomer know that things could never be the same again.

Not half-an-hour of office routine would pass without someone looking sorrowfully at me and murmuring, in a refined sort of *Tatler* voice: 'Tina would have told him to piss off,' 'Tina would have torn it up' or 'Tina wouldn't have read more than three lines before she threw that back.' This would be followed by an exhalation of breath and the hissed words: 'She was brilliant!' One young man in particular (very young, in fact, emotionally a rather nasty eleven-and-a-half by my reckoning) nourished a deep distaste for all women except the departed goddess. 'Tina', he would say, his voice breaking, 'was a very, very warm and motherly person.' Then, apropos something else: 'You shouldn't waste time talking to photographers about frightful pictures. Tina would just have thrown them on the floor. She was – ' Yes, yes, I knew. Brilliant.

Well, I am sure Mr Carter will be able to cope. But the whole problem of coming in from outside to take over from a powerful personality in any business is a fascinating one. I bet it has broken plenty of strong men. It is all right if the departed giant has been a disaster, because you can eclipse him merely by balancing the books and all that they can say, grudgingly, is 'Well, I suppose if you have to have the place run by accountants . . .' But if everything has run smoothly as well as sparkling with the charisma of born leadership, the newcomer has a stark choice. There is absolutely no future in imitation, so he or she must either say in a robust manner 'To hell with Tina, it's my go now'; or else sack half the staff and bring in a gang of old mates. The latter system, much favoured by some incomers, is always an implicit admission of weakness. You know that down in the pub, the old guard are saying 'Tina would never have – ', and there can't be much comfort in huddling up with your few purchased friends meanwhile.

Perhaps he should change the tables and chairs. Furniture can stamp a personality upon an office. To play the part of the delicate escritoire in *Rebecca*, Tina Brown left me an extraordinary round table in the editorial office, next to her own desk. This table, used by visitors to spread out papers and layouts, had an icy marbled top which ensured that anybody who used it for long would develop freezing cold elbows and forearms. I ascribe no actual calculation to my predecessor, but it must be said that it is impossible to drive a hard bargain or argue your corner coherently when you have very cold arms. Perhaps I should have demanded its removal straight away, and replaced it with something that more accurately represented my own management style. An ancient sofa, perhaps, draped in dated antimacassars with the stuffing falling out of it.

Still, if he wants even colder comfort, Mr Carter can reflect on Plomley's Law. This is the phenomenon whereby the person who replaces a revered institution only lasts a short while, absorbing the odium of comparison before giving way to a long-term replacement. Thus Roy Plomley was succeeded by Michael Parkinson on Desert Island Discs: Parkinson drew the flak, clearing the atmosphere for Sue Lawley. And witness the fact that in the recent brouhaha over the *Sunday Times*, people keep saying that Andrew Neil replaced the legendary Harold Evans (Ms Brown's husband), forgetting the existence of Frank Giles. But never mind. To be a buffer, a twilight zone between departing clouds of glory and the light of common day, is an honourable function.

But I would say that, wouldn't I? The marble table and I only lasted six months, and my successor, the late Mark Boxer, was a great hit. I like to think I scuffed the footprints for him.

23

Too darn hot

A referendum on Europe, held in August near Oxford Circus Underground, would turn out a resounding, irrational 'No!' Got enough Europe already, thank you. Europe bumbles around the ticket machines exclaiming in multilingual bafflement, swings its huge rucksack into your face as you struggle by, and blocks your route to work by standing stock-still at the top of the steps, awestruck by the façade of Peter Robinson. To be fair, so do America and Japan. You can tell which is which because the Japanese wear those red shirts with long mad messages beginning BOY GIRL FLYING SWAN LOVE GLORY FLOWER.

But even so, office workers in such tourist honeypot areas would probably not mind the invasion if it were not for the invaders' compulsive habit of pointing them out. 'Voyez!' said a French girl blocking the exit to Tower Hill station. 'Le bowler-hat!' The middle-aged man wearing this rarity scuttled by nervously, past a couple of Germans arguing whether Trinity House was *die Lloyds* or der Bank of England. Meanwhile in ancient university cities across the land, amateur photographers stalk students in gowns, waiting for them to mount bicycles and provide an unforgettable cameo of British life.

And oh, all right, why not? We who are now trying to work while others gawp will, before the summer is out, be doing exactly the same to the picturesque natives of other places. Photographing Irish farmers being gnarled and timeless, perhaps. Or gazing at Greek squid-bashers plying their soggy trade, or embarrassing Provençal villagers by writing winsome books about them. So this is not an insular whinge. I wish to speak up on behalf of all those whose breadwinning becomes a spectator sport. And obviously the plain office commuter is one of the least afflicted: he can sneak indoors and do the actual work in private. Only his journey is recorded, as polite crowds admire his brolly or try to film him on Liverpool Street station as if he were a migrating dungbeetle. Or worse, not film him: last year a New York film crew ordered me to move aside from the crowd because I didn't look typical enough of a British commuter. I think it was the 1972 crinkle-cotton skirt: they're so stylish these Yanks, they couldn't accept it was real. Probably had to go into therapy, later.

The real dread is being looked at while you actually work. It is spreading, and it is high time Zoo Check ran a campaign about it. There are, of course, a few born exhibitionists, closer to the carefree orang-utan than the reticent panda: actors and tennis-players clearly have no desire to keep their grunts private, and building-site workers seem not averse to stripping off their shirts and even responding to scrutiny with a cheery 'Woooaaer!' But even among them there is modesty: why else the little striped tents? Some weed to hide in makes the goldfish life more bearable.

So does prior warning. Everyone can bear to be on show occasionally: the incumbents of 'glamorous' jobs like television vision-mixers or radio presenters get accustomed to being the destination of frequent tour parties. As a Radio 4 Today anchor years ago, I often used to glance up in the middle of a link about the CBI to see a gang of BBC governors and their friends beaming through the glass like exotic tropical fish themselves. But that is all right: you get prior warning (at least, disastrous dressers like me do. They used to say, 'Libby, there's an um, governors' party coming round, perhaps, er . . .' and look at me with big spaniel eyes, hoping that would stop me wearing the POPEYE 'N OLIVE TANGO! sweatshirt and the 1972 skirt, just for one day).

But ever more unwilling exhibits are being dragged into the working zoo. Fishermen and farmers may be resigned to it, as may craftsmen in rural museums who get space to turn a lathe or weave a basket, in return for accepting that if they hit their thumb they must say nothing more contemporary than 'Gadzooks' or 'Begorra!' Waitresses in snack bars who used to be able to go into the kitchen, break wind, eat a leftover frankfurter and do impressions of the customers are now cruelly visible, as they collect food from equally exposed chefs made twitchy at being deprived of their natural right to stick a finger in the soup. Meanwhile at the white-collar end of things, open-plan has forced innocent bank staff to bustle purposefully around in full view of the long queues at the counter.

And the future looks bleak. Already, I am told, the *Los Angeles Times* has become an exhibition newspaper where you can roll up and see real reporters thrillingly drinking coffee out of paper cups. The now abandoned design for a new broadcasting centre at the Langham would have included – it was said – glass walls for the public to peer through, not only at disc jockeys but at respectable middle-aged persons engaged in adding up expenses or writing emollient letters to enraged clergymen about rude words on Loose Ends. A nightmare.

Before any employer moves into this form of tourism, he should think back to the hilarious tours of British Leyland plants conducted by sweating middle-management during the trigger-happy 1970s. What used to happen was that every time your host got nicely into his flow, the line would mysteriously stop and the exhibits – the men on the line – would shrug vague explanations, then look away and grin evilly while the unfortunate middle-manager hustled us visitors back to the office for another look at the new Unipart calendar. Remember one thing, boss-class: a watched pot never boils.

24

Curses!

The question came out of the blue, from the back seat of the car on a school run. 'Mum, why do people in offices swear so much?' I played for time. 'Um – do they?' 'Yes,' said the relentless child. 'Every time I've been into an office ever since I was a baby they're using F words and S words all the time. Why?'

I thought hastily which offices her seven years had taken her into. Not (stop sniggering) all of them BBC or newspaper offices, by any means: what with babysitters showing off their charges to old colleagues, trips behind the scenes to pick up a repaired computer, snippets of television and so forth, the child had seen a fair if fleeting snapshot of office life today. And her conclusion is that people at work are a foul-mouthed bunch. 'You tell us not to swear,' she went on. 'And you tell us that when we're grown up it's good to go to work. So what about us swearing *then*?'

I tried hedging. I said no, no, she must have misheard, I bet they didn't really swear, not with a child there. She was scornful. 'Us being there didn't count,' she said. 'It wasn't *at* us. But while you're yakking to your friends and we look round at the other people because we're bored, there's always someone saying, "Oh Sh—, I haven't phoned Roger," or "F— this b— photocopier," or – ' She was starting to enjoy the licence of quotation rather too much, so I hastily gave in. Yes, darling, I suppose people in offices do swear rather a lot. Not as much as on building sites, perhaps, but more than they used to. I demanded time to cobble up an explanation, and drove on thinking about it.

At the most basic level, it is to do with emphasis, a desire to seem aggressive and dynamic. But it is more than that. I really think office foul-mouthedness contributes to camaraderie: it is a troopship phenomenon. Put a group of people together and they will come up with conventions, tribal signs of recognition, buzzwords. To the reasonably sensitive person, swearing in front of someone else (rather than at them) betokens a certain mutual understanding and trust. If I say 'B— the suppliers' problems, they can b— well get it here on Thursday or I'll rip old Hawkinson's guts out,' I am trusting you to know that I am merely under pressure, and exploding into healthy aggression on behalf of our joint, important effort. You will agree, politely, with me. 'Always were b—tards, those suppliers.'

Some close-knit groups have their own particular pet words, signalling even greater closeness. In one firm a hearty exclamation of 'Arseholes!' may be as routine as the 'ting!' of the telephone; in another, something on the lines of 'Judas!' may suit. On the whole, though, religious blasphemies are shunned in decent offices: real religion might lie deeper than comradeship in some one of those present, but never have been explicitly mentioned because of British reserve; so the rest are careful. Although I did know an innocent lady, a bishop's secretary, who constantly exclaimed 'Oh, bless my buttocks!' when thwarted over some diocesan technicality.

On the whole, the smaller and more isolated the group the worse the language – unless, of course, there is one stickler for decorum in its midst. Boat crews grow alarmingly ripe in their language; so do denizens of small rooms at the end of the corridor where few outsiders ever venture. The presence of customers tones things down a lot, and there is more circumspection in offices which deal with the public on the telephone: you don't want to find yourself relaxing so much that you pick up the phone and snap 'Central blasted Supplies here, how can I help you?' And the presence of women can calm things down too; until they in turn begin to swear freely, and the men relax even more broadly than before, and the whole place starts to sound like an alternative cabaret night in a cellar at the Edinburgh Festival.

And then someone who used to work there years ago drops in with her innocent, wide-eared toddler, and the ingrained habit causes scandal (and much pleasure) to the little one.

So I don't know what to tell her. It clearly isn't true to say that only nasty, coarse, violent people swear. Nor to take the more modern line that only unimaginative and stupid people do it because they don't know many words. If that were so, why is the air in newspaper offices so blue? And how do you account for all those terminally unimaginative and verbally inept people who never swear at all, even to say *bum*?

So I gave up. 'I don't really know why they do. Silly, isn't it?'

She snorted in amused contempt. 'When I have an office,' she observed, 'I'm going to make a rule that people have got to swear. Then they probably won't do it.' I think this child has potential.

25

The Cliff Wright Solution

*L*istless, dejected, fed up? Back from holiday and hating it? Or worse, are you sharing an office with someone who has just had his three weeks in the Dordogne and now sports a glowing carcinogenic suntan and expression of intense sullenness? Take heart. I offer you, free of charge, the Cliff Wright Solution.

Mr Wright, now honourably retired, used to be the Chief Engineer at Radio Oxford, and as such he had a good deal to put up with. Upon BBC local radio engineers falls the task of absorbing and buffering the tensions and shocks which occur when engineering facts meet creative ideas, feasibility clashes with the urgent dreams of newsmen, and middle-aged engineers in ties who enjoy Nevil Shute confront illiterate juveniles with their knuckles brushing the ground. When the Radio Car broke down during an interview about the Watchfield Free Festival with Airey Neave MP and a hippie organizer stranded in it, not speaking; when Magdalen College Tower required 150 ft of cable dangling down its ancient sides to convey the dawn carol on Mayday, and the cable began picking up World Service; or when a circus bear ate my microphone windshield, we all brought our little troubles to Cliff and his colleague Derek. Usually, they kept smiling.

But once he had a long-service sabbatical and went away for several months. When he came back, Mr Wright looked around with some distaste and formulated a principle I have never forgotten. 'There ought to be a rule,' he said. 'When you get back to work, you should be entitled in your contract to one full day's sulking for each week you've been away.'

It was brilliant. Think about it: after a long weekend you could legitimately remain dopey and unproductive until Tuesday midday (you will anyway, so you might as well have it as a right). After a fortnight off, you need barely speak to your colleagues until Wednesday. After a month, you get four days' recuperation when your mind can be visibly elsewhere, your lunch-hours evasively lengthened and your telephone callers fobbed off with impunity. After maternity leave you would have a full fortnight in which to behave as badly as you wish. Just think of it: none of that showy dynamism and brittle pretended enthusiasm, none of those tight Lycra skirts to prove to the boss you ain't a back number yet. You could stick with your floral sacks, riffle through beloved photographs all day with favoured colleagues, shove the URGENT pile into the drawer and lope off home to the baby at 4.15, without even bothering to mutter some lie about a dental appointment. And nobody could interfere with your legitimate sulking-period. But when it ended you would be expected to snap back into full productivity, willingness and humming energy.

. They really might as well write it into employment law, this compassionate-leave-of-your-senses, because few of us come back from holiday entirely normal. Nor is it a charter for lead-swingers and idlers, because in fact the habitual idler comes back more predictable – still idle and sulky – than the dedicated workaholic. Everybody has higher expectations of the latter, but the fact is that once a conscientious, nitpicking office worrier does actually succeed in switching off (and it can take days of pacing the beach sands worrying about the restructuring of the Middle East branch), it is equally difficult to switch him on again. He – or she – looks at the same worn carpet, the same peeling year-planners, the same telephone grimed with the panic grip of old deadlines, and feels the creeping horror of an addict looking back on his old degradation. The sight is about as welcome as handcuffs to a freed hostage, or a full ashtray to a reformed smoker. When you have experienced being another and younger man, or a happy and carefree woman, for a fortnight the very sight of the office can hit you like a physical blow. You get over it, and shrug on the old yoke eventually with resignation, but it takes time. Sulking time. So why not make it official, like trauma leave? You are in grief, mourning your holiday self.

Perhaps they should also hand out a few little texts to read during the days of yawning. There is a very splendid one from Jonathan Gathorne-Hardy quoted in the new *Chatto Book of Office Life*.

'No-one ever seriously believes', says Mr Gathorne-Hardy, 'that they will be in an office all their working lives. For forty-five years. Secretly they believe something will rescue them – a football pool, arson. "I'm sorry, sir. Yes, completely burnt to the ground. As you see, sir, just a gaping hole. Not a hope of it starting up again, I'm afraid. All the files gone, the records – the whole Board consumed in the flames too, I'm afraid. But I understand they were well insured, very well insured. Compensation should amount to three-quarters full salary for the rest of each employee's lifetime. Yes, quite sure, sir." '

Sharing this fantasy unhindered, just for those few sulking days, might make all the difference. Then the blazing holiday light will pale, the office furniture cease to look so like a rack and screw, and the returned sulker turn into a reasonably committed colleague again. It is Wright's Law. Let it be recognized.

26

Nightmares

*T*here is nothing like a sharp dose of summer flu and deliri-
ous nightmares to bring working life into perspective. A
mad perspective, of course, but nonetheless interesting. Sweating
through half-sleep over the last two days I have entertained in
quick succession all the old horror classics.

There is the one about trying to read a newspaper while all the
print cascades off on to the floor, tinkling nonsensically. There
is the old favourite from local radio days, in which I am a
disc-jockey trying to play 'Long-Haired Lover from Liverpool'
but then I look down and the record has turned into a Lyons
Individual Blackberry and Apple Pie, and the needle is graunching
through the pastry with a shower of sugary flakes and a loud
Scchhhrrrrrr noise and I am powerless to take it off. There is
the one where I open a magazine and read a piece under my
name and photograph which I can't remember writing, but which
roundly libels both Sir James Goldsmith and the Princess Royal, and
warmly advocates vivisection of furry animals. And this morning,
crashing out again in a penicillin haze, I even dreamed the rarest
of the lot, for me: the one where I am host of a live radio
programme with a tableful of people, and have not the faintest
idea who any of them are. In a variant of this dream they are
all bishops except one, and I keep calling the wrong one 'Bishop'
and the others say in chorus 'No, I'm the bishop' and then I say,
'Well, in any case, the issue we're discussing is –' and I can't
remember what the hell it is, and everyone stares at me. And I

hand over to Continuity, and wake up drenched and shaking in the dark.

I suppose everyone has nightmares about work. All those New Age dream analysts who drone on about dreams betokening sexual insecurities or a need to reconcile yourself to your star sign are way off-beam. They are out of date, stuck in a time when women had the vapours and no jobs to go to. Sexual insecurities and life changes are small potatoes compared to the massive influence of work. Of course we dream about work: it occupies an immense amount of our lives and emotional energies. And of course we have nightmares about it: after all, work by its very nature presents to the busy subconscious such an immense number of openings for nightmare that it would be criminal on the part of that subconscious to waste the opportunity for mayhem by night.

It starts young. Babies wake up flailing their arms and crying 'Can't hit-a-peg!' if they have been having trouble with their hammer-peg toys. My son regularly dreams that he has turned up at his new school wearing the wrong uniform. Students dream about trying to write an exam paper with invisible ink, or underwater, or up the sides of blades of grass. Pregnant women dream (well, I did) that the baby emerges complete with a detailed instruction booklet, all in Japanese. Farmers at this time of year stumble in their sleep through nightmare threatening fields of wheat, and dream that bits keep falling off their combine harvester (and wake up, like the Old Man of Peru, to find it is perfectly true).

But for the subconscious working mind, the more surreally horrible, the better. I suppose bankers with flu dream that they have lent money to Robert Maxwell and lost the receipt. And doctors hear their bleepers and can't find them under billowing nightmare operating gowns. And editors, no doubt, toss uneasily in a nocturnal conviction that they have landed themselves with another set of Hitler Diaries, made of jelly and rapidly melting in the sun.

Pause for another hot, confused sleep. This time, I swear it, I dreamed that I was ordered to write a five-part series on Gnats. I begin 'Gnats, frankly, are no joke' and can't get further. This will not do. I must readjust these dreams to be of positive use, rather than wholly demoralizing. I must be like Lorna.

Lorna used to work in an office I spent some time in, and her speciality was coming in at nine o'clock, fixing some colleague with a soulful blue eye and delivering the unanswerable opening line, 'Ooh, I dreamed about you last night.' If male, the colleague would start to preen hopefully. We females merely looked, understandably, hunted. Lorna had a way of drawing you into a horrible cloying intimacy through these alleged dreams, as a result of which she got away with murder on every other front. When someone, otherwise a mere nodding acquaintance, has just confided that she spent the night riding side-by-side with you on white horses through surf, it is extremely difficult to round on her and tell her to re-type the last six letters with more conventional spelling. If you have, all unwillingly, been lured into a Scheherazade session about how she dreamed you were going to tea with the Queen, only you didn't have any clothes so she wove you some out of spiders' webs, it is not easy to take a firm line when the mysterious Seer extends her lunch-hour until 3.30. What is more, if anyone was unpleasant to Lorna, she would come in and say, 'Ooh, I dreamed about you last night,' in a meaningful tone and then add, 'but it was a bit awful, so I'd better not say.' The victim spent the rest of the day avoiding walking under ladders and wishing he or she had a lucky rabbit's foot handy.

Yes, that is the way to do it. Ignore the real, murky, tangled, miserably insecure dreams and make up a whole fresh set, for public consumption, self-glorification and one-upmanship. As the old advertisements nearly used to put it, *I dreamed I was writing for the London Times – in my Maidenform Bra!* And not about gnats, either.

27

Sick notes, sour notes

Now that we are all heartily sick of the details of other people's marital shenanigans, there is a gap to be filled. I mean to say, do you seriously want to read *one more word* about toes, Texans, or teenage stepdaughters? We have heard it all. We need something else to replace the entertainment which used to be found in really dirty divorce-court reporting. And I reckon we have found it: industrial tribunals.

Like fragments of soap opera they let us peep briefly inside the tangled emotional world of other people's offices. From a position of safety we share the passions which seethe around directorial car-parking ('She had been warned about parking in my space!' – 'Well, I got in earlier than him!'); over the length of lunch-hour, the interpretation of office compliments and the complex unwritten code of perks and expenses. We can appreciate the way resentful paranoia can fix itself on to the telephone manner of a colleague, or her pet Shi-Tzu. These emotions are usually as private as marriage itself, but like the old fault-finding divorce cases, these unfair dismissal tribunals make both sides fight hard, dirty and detailed.

This week's pearl was the case of the British Telecom maintenance engineer who appears to hold the world record for sick leave. The tribunal was told that one domestic accident knocked the complainant out for 227 days, food poisoning for 26, a 'bad cold' for 25, and so forth. He lost his specific claim for unfair dismissal when it turned out he had not been dismissed at all, but consented to early retirement ('It is clear that my client has been less than frank with me,' said his lawyer, through gritted teeth). But what sticks in the mind is the last word of the complainant. 'I felt I had a case, but it didn't come out as it should have,' he said. 'They had always wanted to get rid of me. It was as simple as that.'

Ah yes! That is the way it is, all right. When you are a virtuoso wielder of sick-notes, the distasteful fact is that employers do want to get rid of you. Fast. Indeed, they wish they had never hired you. You are not an asset. You wreck rotas, sabotage shift planning and mess up their clients. This may seem unkind when your dropped arches are giving you such hell, but it is harsh commercial fact: from a practical point of view, you stink.

It takes time, of course, to reach this point. Your first bout of flu may attract genuine sympathy. Your subsequent windsurfing injury might meet nothing more than tolerant derision, and your first few migraine attacks provoke only a silent, thoughtful neutrality. But if you take it further, and contrive to fall off the kitchen stool while putting up a Venetian blind, contract five distinct mystery viruses and develop a tendency to lower back pain, the employer will become downright hostile. A coherent, recurring illness is often tolerated: I know of companies which have nursed increasingly disabled employees with something akin to family love. What drives employers and colleagues barking mad is the unconnected, random string of sickies. Even when they are immaculately authenticated.

Most of us know this perfectly well. We operate a private system of checks and balances: when we wake up feeling rotten we instantly compute whether or not we are entitled to. 'Hmmm,' we say, 'I haven't been off sick for years, I had the hysterectomy in my summer holidays and I did nights of overtime on the Dutch contract. I'm staying in bed.' Or else: 'Better stagger in, it's only three weeks since I had the shingles and George handled all my stuff then . . .' It is not wholly rational, but it keeps things ticking over. Indeed I once stumbled from hospital straight into the BBC in thick sunglasses after double eye surgery, for no better reason than that I was plotting to bunk out of a programme the following month to go ski-ing. So I swopped my sickie for a skive. Fair enough.

But some never make this calculation. They succumb to every passing breeze with a sense of utter justification which drives their paymasters mad. We had a nanny once who – when not suffering from 'One of my dropped throats' or 'The back thing again' – devoted three weeks a month to pre-menstrual tension and the remaining week to nervous exhaustion. 'Anaemic symptoms,' she would murmur to my husband. 'It was a very heavy flow – ' Exit husband, flinching, as Nanny packed for another long weekend. I am convinced she believed passionately in her own suffering. I am also convinced that 99 per cent of humanity regularly works through worse.

But how, asks the desperate employer, can one spot these frail vessels at the interview? Unless they actually fall over the carpet or use a throat spray between sentences? The only suggestion I can offer is from a Machiavellian recruiting interviewer who sometimes resorts to taking a pill herself in mid-interview, and sneezingly mentions some nebulous ailment. Then she waits to see if the candidate is interested. If he or she starts peering at the medicine and saying, 'Oooh, yes, I get that . . .', it is blue-pencil time.

Take note, job-hunters. Next time your interviewer succumbs to violent coughing, it may be a trick. Remember to look baffled, healthy, and bored by such frailty. You'll get the job.

28

Putting off the Ritz

D readful, dreadful news from the Ritz Hotel. I hate to black-
guard the dear old Ritz, because (not a lot of people know
this) I used to edit its guest magazine. I spent many a happy hour
copying out interesting facts about rococo gilding methods, and
chewing the fat below stairs with amiable housekeepers, Palm Court
waiters and vintage porters. I also conducted a set-piece interview
for each issue over a sumptuous lunch in its restaurant. And believe
me, until you have shared a grouse with Jeffrey Archer and quizzed
Sarah Brightman by the soft light of a crêpe Suzette, you haven't
lived. The interviews weren't so hot (those done over meals rarely
are, because the journalist gets so bored transcribing tapesful of
clattering and glugging), but the food was immaculate.

And this relates to my dreadful news. The Ritz has devised a new
award scheme. It plans to name the Business Luncher of the Year, or
'the executive who does most to help the recovery of the economy
by lunching out.' The winner will have spent at least £5,000 a year
at the trough, and 'be known personally to six head waiters'. What he
or she must be known for is not stipulated. Presumably the winner
should not be quite as rash as the chap who lately got sacked for
running up a bill of £448 for two at the Gavroche because his
employers, rather plaintively, said that his expenses and his taste
for wine at £119.50 a bottle were 'inappropriate to a registered
charity with severe cash-flow difficulties'.

The trouble is that once you have an award scheme for something,
it takes on *gravitas*. Why else do haberdashers and tobacconists set

up Tieman and Pipeman awards, and jeans manufacturers celebrate the Rear of the Year? The Ritz award, whether we like it or not, confers a certain fresh lustre on the revolting practice of business lunching, just when some of us hoped it was dying out under the onslaught of health nannies and One Minute Managers. People will compete for this award, showing off and sucking up to head waiters in a horrible fashion, twinkling ostentatiously over the thin mints and sending compliments to the chef. And their guests, or victims, will sit gloomily crumbling bread and reflecting that they could have sewn the whole deal up in twenty minutes over a plate of sandwiches with the right files handy, and got home early that night with a calm stomach.

I hate business lunches. They rattle me. Lunch I love, and business I love, but not at the same time. Sharing food is a gentle, undemanding, affectionate human activity. Doing business is something quite different. Mixing them goes against nature. Do lions determine their territory while sharing a carcass by a waterhole? Do wildebeeste or kudu attempt to graze together while in the process of locking horns in combat? They do not. They separate the two activities. They have got some sense. Speaking as a woman with pigs, I can tell you that when two of them lunch together, it is not a sociable or constructive activity. They gobble in silence, fight over the last slop, and only then shamble off to a far corner to get on with the joint project of digging up the fence-posts. Business and food are a poor mix.

With one important exception. I do not include as business lunches the kind of amiable, celebratory meals in which one indulges with colleagues – or bosses – with whom one's relationship is signed and sealed. They are all right. They put professional relationships on a personal basis, and the bestowal of food therefore resumes its primitive and correct symbolic overtones of affection. Your Chairman or MD, publisher or editor is as it were, breast-feeding you. You are bonding. The one snag here is that although such bonding experiences are chargeable to expenses, it would be hard to claim that they do much for the UK economy, since the actual work has already been signed for, and if truth be told you both ought to be back in the office, doing it.

No: the real horror is the true business meal, the manipulative lunch. Someone's secretary rings up and asks you to go, and being too craven or well-mannered to ask 'What exactly is this lunch *about?'* – well, it offends deep instincts of courtesy to question a fellow-being's offer to share his bone – you put it in your diary. If you are a supplier, or a headhunter, or a company being stalked by a bigger company, you may have a general idea of what is coming. But the host's intention is not to get to the point until you have eaten his bread and salt, and thereby put yourself in his debt. Therefore you don't enjoy the starter or the small-talk, and you eat too many breadsticks and feel sick.

Then the host gets to the point, somewhere between the sauté potatoes and the coffee. If you are lucky, the key line – 'We were wondering, back in the office, if you weren't feeling a bit overstretched' or 'Have you ever considered a merger?' – occurs during the entrée, allowing you at least some digestive scope. If you are with a masterful and experienced business-luncher, it may be thin-mint time before he comes to the crunch. And if his proposal is too unspeakable even to consider ('We feel you might have just that light yet sympathetic touch needed to ghost the Duchess's book on her battle against cellulite'), how are you going to say so? When you've just eaten seventy-five quidsworth of his budget?

Horrible, horrible. Could one, perhaps, win the award if one was personally known to six head waiters for one's habit of fainting dead away over the prawns and having to be stretchered to the Ladies?

29

Heads are rolling

I am uneasy. Institutions are crumbling right and left, shedding magic and majesty. *Things fall apart, the centre cannot hold*; instead of respecting the old and serviceable conjuring-tricks which have cemented the nation together for decades, a new brash generation is saying 'Phooey! I don't believe in fairies!' and sending countless venerable Tinkerbelles crashing to the ground. Nervous traditionalists fear that they will never revive.

Some will, of course. When I talk of things crumbling I do not refer to the House of Windsor. That House knows perfectly well what to do in a crisis: close your ears, cram on a petal hat, keep opening hospitals and going to church; and bingo! come Remembrance Sunday everyone will have forgotten all the fuss. But there are less resilient institutions which have lately lost their Edwardian shine and sureness: Lloyds of London, the City, British Rail, Farming, the Police, the BBC . . .

And now, heaven help us, there is a trend for knocking public-school headmasters and headmistresses off their perches. Three famous ones have gone down in the last month: the Dragon School in Oxford shed its new Headmaster, Helen Williams ceased abruptly to be High Mistress of St Paul's, and at Haberdashers' Monmouth School for Girls there were reportedly 'important differences of view' between headteacher and governors which climaxed in the head being slung out like some Victorian tweeny who broke a plate too many.

I suppose these may all have been good decisions: outsiders

cannot know. It is also dangerous to generalize on relations between governors and headteachers, because there is only so much time in the day for answering intemperate letters, and both classes of person, in my bitter experience, produce a fair quorum of logorrhoeic stinkers only too ready to fall on the Basildon Bond and excoriate journalists ('Copy to Editor' they write on the top, 'Copy to Director-General of the BBC, Copy to Archbishop of Canterbury', etc.). So never mind the politicians: just consider the question of whether the holders of certain respected jobs – headteachers, bishops, generals, deans, directors-general, and editors of literate periodicals – ought really to be so vulnerable to abrupt public dismissal.

If they do something scandalous, fine. When a Director of Public Prosecutions resigns after being caught kerb-crawling, we can talk comfortably about tragic flaws and the pressure of office. But suppose a DPP was kicked out merely because he wasn't quite the tone of DPP the appointing elders fancied – that would be different, wouldn't it? It would give the public a sense that someone was tinkering, messing about, doodling on the canvas of public life.

When a headteacher, for example, has committed no obvious crime, there is something uneasy about this weaselly talk of 'differences of view' and 'resignations by mutual agreement'. There always is, in such lofty and respectworthy jobs. It raises the question of why the Governors (or Trustees, or Privy Council, or Synod, or whoever) were such twerps as to appoint this person in the first place. Such bodies should look around at the racketier sections of society, and notice what happens – for instance – in the media. When magazines and newspapers start to get through editors like Kleenex, or television programmes hype a wonderful new presenter and sack her in six months, nobody wins. Onlookers merely write off the management as a bunch of headless chickens, and talented candidates veer off, concluding that an approach from this organization is not unlike a proposal of marriage from Henry VIII.

To counter this, the appointing body must headhunt and cajole and flatter, exaggerating the shortcomings of the departing postholder and laying out their stall enticingly. Which is not the way to recruit someone of the high ideals and private certainties which once (we hoped, and liked to believe) distinguished the great and the good. Remember Lord Reith in 1922, striding into the BBC with a conviction that God had sent him? The Company may have quailed in subsequent months, but they gave him his head and let him grow. Even the great need backing up.

And we need the great: the difficult, the idiosyncratic, the visionary. Remarkable individuals need to be spotted and nurtured by committees of the wise. Kind readers have been sending me more examples of the last words of advice spoken by legendary headteachers, and I must say these gain a lot of gravitas from having been uttered by that generation of heads who nobody would have dared to contemplate sacking over 'differences of view'. So far my favourites are 'If you catch yourself behaving like a shopgirl, read a Shakespeare sonnet' (Roedean, allegedly), 'Never touch gin or Polish Officers' (Cheltenham Ladies' College, 1943), and the Yorkshire Reverend Mother who told her girls, 'Always put something aside for unexpected tax demands.' Where Rev. Mother got it from is a mystery. Some pupil's ruined father, probably. But it stuck with my correspondent for life.

Still, the world of disposable, sackable, forgettable pillars of society may have its advantages. When the furious letters come in (*Copy to DG, copy to Editor, copy to Cardinal Hume*) I shall at least be able to console myself with the reflection that by the time they get their copies all three might be down at the Jobcentre with me.

30

Name of the game

*T*here was another of those dopey surveys the other day about what your name does to you. If you are Elizabeth, Rose, Emily or Lucy, suggests a Sussex University researcher, you will end up feminine, soft and sensitive and ladylike. If you are called Lesley or Robyn you won't.

There will, of course, be dissent. Heck, I was christened Elizabeth Mary, and everybody knows that after the first fifteen pints of lager I love to bend iron bars with my teeth. And I bet you know at least one Rose who spits rivets and eats grown men for breakfast. Anyway, as far as my own formidable child Rose (as ladylike as a Landrover so far) keeps reminding me, the name originates in the Old Norse *hros*, meaning horse, not flower. So there.

But this is a shallow age, and Sussex University students are clearly well in touch with its essential beliefs: one of which is that names will magically alter natures. Once it was only actors who really believed this, refusing point-blank to be Micklewhite or Fluck if there was the option of Caine or Dors. But the rot has spread farther. They know this up at Windscale – um, Sellafield. And at Talbot, BT, and Relate. Hitherto dignified and impregnable professions have begun to take the message on board too: I met a trainee teacher who was seriously advised at college to consider working under a pseudonym lest she provoke 'negative or distracting' reactions from her pupils because her surname was Balls. 'Take off the"s" ', her supervisor suggested, 'in everybody's interest.' Ms Balls proudly refused. She, like me, grew up in an era when a teacher was not afraid to face a class simply because her name was Mrs Haddock. But she was out of step with the times.

Nowhere is the mania for cosmetic re-naming more evident than in job descriptions. I do not wish to sound like some old Garrick Club fossil, but as a lover of plain language I do hark back with a certain wistfulness to the days of stewards and bailiffs, clerks and ratcatchers and treasurers. And, indeed, jobbing builders who did not feel the need to waste money on cards saying *Building Maintenance Services, JM Bloggs (Working Director)*. But it is hard, now, to see the way back.

I suppose it must have occurred to somebody one day that names cost less than pay rises. It certainly occurred in the world of magazines, which have now sprouted so many Editors that it is almost chic *not* to have the magic E-word in your title. What the hell does a Consulting Editor actually edit? Or a Contributing Editor? Is there a Cleaning Editor who goes around with a mop at six o'clock? Is it better to be an Assistant Editor or an Associate Editor? (don't answer that, best not to know). On such periodicals the real Editor is renamed Editor-in-Chief, with all the grandiose military and Red Indian implications that carries (How! Editor-in-Chief, him drink firewater with braves).

Other trades have been quick to latch on. I trained at the BBC as a Programme Operations Assistant, and was quite pleased to be so designated. Especially as my actual skills often made me more of a Programme Operations Impediment, unplugging the wrong bits at the wrong moment. Halfway through my first year, however, it was decided that we had better rise to the status of Studio Managers. A lot of secretaries were meanwhile renamed Production Assistants (one school of thought murmured about Production Assistance Managers). And so it went on, everyone's description inflating.

Business was already junking managers by 1980, in favour of Executives. Curiously, the older title often endured at the very top – a Bank Manager staying the same, but his undermanager mutating into a Special Account Executive or the like. Local authorities developed a great weakness for militaria, with everything from Pest Control Officers, commanding squads of unruly silverfish and maggots, to Recreation Officers ('by the left – platoon – Relax!'). Many have now, interestingly, gone back to managers again. Elsewhere, everyone scrambled to be either a 'Head of' something (implying great seniority, even if you are only head of one disgruntled secretary and a broken photocopier) or else an Analyst (implying that you stand a bit aloof from the rest of the organization, telling it where it goes wrong). Names provide enhanced self-image, definition, camouflage, prestige: especially with pompous clients, who wouldn't deal with an undermanager anyway. All for free. Yippee!

But beware of the heritage era. The cachet of ancient names grows ever stronger, and those who never changed are growing smug. Oxford colleges are pretty pleased with themselves for still having 'scouts' to clean the rooms, instead of Student Hygiene Executives. Organizations with financial Comptrollers feel somehow more secure in a recession, more in comptrol perhaps. Trinity House is pretty happy to have Elder Brethren, and hard-nosed City businessmen scheme and ache for the chance to be Worshipful Saddlemakers or Honourable Watermen, as they yearn back to the days of comprehensible trades.

And who would not pity the winner of the job advertised last week in this newspaper: Head of Fundraising at one of the oldest Oxford colleges. How is this poor devil going to hold his head up in the senior common-room? Could they not at least call him the Regius Head of Fundraising?

31

Nostalgie de la boot

*T*here is something touching about Paddy Ashdown's stated resolution to go forth among the workers and try being ordinary. My colleague Matthew Parris reported last week that the Leader began on a building site in Harrogate, wearing a helmet and crinkling his eyes up at lumps of reinforced concrete. Oh, how they mock, these political commentators! But I am with Paddy, for he stands in a proud tradition. Not a terribly useful one, on the whole, but a proud one nevertheless. And I have been there too. I tell you, he is going to have *fun*.

Attempting to share the life of the manual worker – the male manual worker in particular – is one of the oldest sports of the British intelligentsia. Ever since the nation divided into whey-faced white-collar types with typewriters and gnarled muscular hewers of wood and drawers of water, the ones with clean soft hands have been gazing wistfully over the fence. Writers and artists, politicians and Princes of Wales have been overcome with *nostalgie de la boot*, and itched to pull a pair on, don moleskin trousers, roll up their sleeves and join in. For a bit, anyway. Just for long enough to get something picturesque for the book-jacket blurb.

The manual worker, meanwhile, remains strangely unmoved by this charade. If he is a brickie or a ploughman or a waiter, he already knows what it is like and doesn't particularly want to read about it. Nor does he wish to entrust the laying of the next course of bricks, the drawing-out of a stetch or the serving of scampi to some shining-faced amateur fresh off a creative writing course.

Most particularly he does not relish the idea of being described as 'a twisted giant of a man' or 'prematurely grey, but with his own dignity'. He wants to finish work and go home. On time.

The visitor, on the other hand, wants to get high on the Dignity Of Labour. In the revolutionary sixties it was *de rigueur* for the politically OK Oxford undergraduate to be a dustman in his holidays. We girls mainly stuck to waitressing, but the thrill was adulterated by the uneasy suspicion that the world being what it is, we might end up as real waitresses, degree and all. But both sexes united in scorn of wimps who spent their vacation being researchers for MPs, or pushing pens in Daddy's office.

Some amateurs and writers, like Orwell among the *plongeurs*, have traded places to pretty good effect: but all are tainted by the very fact that they weren't bred to it, don't have to do it and can go back anytime. And if by chance they can't, they are probably by that time surrounded by kindred spirits: I remember when graduate unemployment was just invented my younger brother's exasperated riposte to a worried parent. 'Oh don't worry, Dad – I mean, I've got the worst degree of all the porters at Harvey Nichols!' But in the case of writers, politicians, princes, ideological slummers and other tourists their interlude of manual work is at best a safari, and at worst a theme park.

I know. I did it for years. It began as a mere escape route. Arriving on local radio to find myself expected to be interested in playgroups and cooking, I fled precipitately in the opposite direction, and insisted on making a gritty series of work portraits featuring jobs as macho as possible. Goodness, it was fun. I rattled through the dawn on a Travelling Post Office train. I climbed up a 100 ft tower crane with a tape recorder to interview the crane driver (unfortunately his best stories got cut out for reasons of national security. The crane happened to overlook the prison exercise yard and he saw a lot of things).

I sheared a sheep. I was a removal man for a day – well, I got in the way of some removal men actually, but Paddy and I do mean well, we really do. I drove to Kent overnight in a lorryful of racing pigeons, and swept a chimney. I went out with the sewermen. One day when we were cleaning out a blocked septic tank at a grand riverside house (with the usual merry running commentary on the householders' diet and habits) the lady of the house popped out with our tea. I actually knew her, but in overalls I passed unrecognized. 'Does the boy take sugar, too?' she fluted. The men exchanged glances, feeling by this time entitled to their bit of fun. 'Yeh, you do, don't'cha, Sid?' Sid I remained for the rest of the day, and it was better than a BAFTA.

I recommend it to any politician, in power or out. Go for it. Get some brick-dust in your wrinkles. It may not save the nation, but it beats wrestling with a kamikaze pound. And you can always have the chauffeur waiting in case it palls.

32

Backlash brooding

I shall always remember where I was on the day the new sins came in. I was at a conference on women and employment, convened by *She* magazine, and was just hauling some notes out of my briefcase when my eye fell on the headline about the newly leaked Roman Catholic catechism, complete with modern sins such as drunken driving, reading horoscopes, and forging cheques. Pausing only to marvel that a catechism could be secret enough to be 'leaked' (is your damnation embargoed if you do them meanwhile? Do we have two months' grace in which to read Gipsy Petulengro without fear?) I indulged in a brief Garrickish snort about there being surely nothing left uncovered by the old concepts like chastity, charity and false idols anyway, and stuffed it back. Then I went in to listen to a fascinating series of lectures on cultural trends, marketing, whether women managers are more sensitive (consensus: yes, but it's nothing to be smug about) and how advertisers see them (dangly earrings, power hairdos and lousy tempers, mainly).

By the end of the day, on the train home, I was ready to read it properly. I must admit I had rather hoped for some up-to-the-minute new sins such as deliberately fomenting war between the sexes, panic selling of currencies, telephoto snapping and taking free holidays off infidels. Alas, none were there. However, Slander is now joined by 'manipulating public opinion', which should wipe out politicians and journalists (with the possible exception of those who merely assault it without effect).

But then my mind veered back to the conference, and the always fascinating insights of the marketeers. Did you know that just-add-water cake mix was a failure, but that when they changed the formula so you had to beat in an egg, women bought it because they felt they were still really cooking? That you can't sell doors if your ad shows them closed, because Anglo-Saxon babies are traumatized by their mothers putting them in their cots and closing the door? If you want to sell doors photograph them ajar, preferably with Mummy on her way back in. I love these marketing theories. It seems a shame that the ingenious people who discover them should be damned for manipulation. But then, all advertising is based on the seven deadly sins: I used to play a private game on the Underground escalators, gliding past the posters spotting the sins incited, at speed: 'Gluttony, gluttony, lust, lust, envy, covetousness, lust, gluttony – er – pride – ' and so on. Try it sometime.

Sin and work, sin and work. My mind spun (I am by now, remember, sitting on a lumpy briefcase on the floor of a packed commuter train inching towards Colchester, with the weary snore of the men of Essex all around). The conference on working women had come as something of a surprise. Five years ago, any such gathering would have been exclusively about equal pay, glass ceilings, flexitime, harassment, childcare, etc. If things of the heart and spirit came into it, they would have been exclusively concerned with women's feelings, the need for self-esteem and the benefits of networking. It would have been, in other words, prickly with envy, covetousness, anger, and pride.

But this wasn't. Call it the caring nineties if you like, call it the New Age or the feminist backlash, but the day was quite different in tone to anything which would have attracted the same mix of successful women in the 1980s. One male speaker related with some passion the story of his own father's life sacrificed to conventional workaholic behaviour, and declared himself much happier and more of a family man since he lost his main job. He pleaded with women not to make the same mistake. The floor applauded and me, I nearly went straight home to bake some hominy grits. A flamboyantly feminine Brazilian-born pundit traced the behaviour of working women firmly back to biology and culture, not to mention nursery doors. It was hard to remember the days when anyone saying 'Biology is destiny' used to get wine flung in his face. Whenever flexible working or humane management were mentioned, everyone immediately pointed out the advantage to both sexes and murmured 'paternity leave, so important'. A female haulage executive reported that her women's network in the West Country now invited men to its meetings.

It was, in short, much less slanderously, manipulatively, angrily, proudly sinful than these things used to be.

And if any of the Essex chaps had got up and offered me a turn in his seat, I wouldn't have turned on him with feminist scorn and shrieked 'Body fascist!' I would have taken it.

But none of them did.

33

Fun at the TV factory

One of the great British failings, we are told, is that we don't respect our manufacturing industry. 1986 was Industry Year, full of campaigns and words of praise for the dynamic future of British manufacturing, but a recent survey showed that 83 per cent of us didn't even know it was happening. For a nation that is supposed to be pitching for a new industrial revolution, we seem to be remarkably lacking in grass-roots enthusiasm.

Or so it seems, unless you happen to share a house with anyone under five. The toddlers, I can report, are absolutely wonderful. They walk around all day, punching imaginary clocks and chanting:

> Packing and stacking, no we don't believe in slacking
> We're Nell and Flo and we're always on the go.

Their entire lives have been taken over by Bertha the Big Machine. Bertha is a big green machine with multicoloured cogwheels, a computer panel and a friendly smile, who lives in a factory called Spottiswood and Co. and is tended by dumpy little puppets. She is a BBC children's television programme, she is a stack of books, she is a cassette of remorseless, repetitive songs.

Before Bertha, if you were two or three years old, you were encouraged to model yourself on a rural postman in the Yorkshire dales – good old Postman Pat bumbling around wasting Post Office time by pulling sheep out of fences. After Bertha my small son wore a tea cosy on his head and claimed to be a Sikh forklift driver called Panjit from Stores, and my two-year-old daughter alternated between the packing and stacking department and the demanding role of Mrs Tupp the tea-lady. They are as happy as Japanese workers, singing the company song:

> Getting to work on Monday never seems too hard
> When you know you've got your workmates waiting
> When you've punched your card

When your baby lisps out 'Just off to the design office, mummy,' and your four-year-old frowns into his clipboard (he begged for one) and mutters 'I've an order here from Spengler's that needs seeing to,' things are getting serious. We begin to suspect some fiendish intelligence up at the CBI is at work, forcing us willy-nilly to nurture the industrial generation of the next century.

'I'm the foreman,' said my son loudly, one day. 'Back to work, everybody.' And his little sister, once so rebellious, put down her doll's cup, hitched up her nappy, and crouched over the toy cogwheels with ferocious concentration. She was singing something, so I leaned towards her and caught a few lines of the apprentice's song in which the boy sits 'dweaming of de day his name will be – on de manager's door!'

There is a thoroughly CBI atmosphere of purposefulness in the plots. Machine minders eat their sandwiches next to the conveyor belt, while earnestly discussing problems of design and production.

Life at Spottiswood and Co. is not quite as gritty as reality, of course. When the song says that the manager 'has in store a surprise for the shopfloor', it does not mean massive redundancies and thousands of latex puppets on the scrap-heap; he is merely having a birthday party for Bertha the Big Machine.

These days, when we wake, the little workers have taken to chanting the Manager's Song by heart:

> Mr Willmake will make sure orders coming through the door
> Will be treated as they should up at Spot-tis-wood
> Getting orders out on time with his smooth production line . . .

It is like having Sir Terence Beckett singing down the baby alarm at you. Their voices rise to a crescendo, extolling the proud history of their company and praising the management as good workers must:

His family pictures on the wall looking down on him
Remind us of the past they all went out to win
Making Spottiswood the place where orders kept on rolling in
It's just the same today, it's just the same today
And good old Mr Willmake making sure it stays that way!

I look rather wistfully, now, at old Postman Pat under the sofa.
They'll be privatizing him next.

34

On the hype road to fame

Greatness is within everybody's reach: all it takes is salesmanship, it appears.

Once, self-improvement books were about efficiency and organization. Next they were about winning friends and manipulating people, 'having it all' or being a 'one-minute manager'. For a while now they have been about inner fulfilment, with instructions on how to seek your true self through celibacy, or odd eating habits, or aromatic acupressure. Now connoisseurs of the genre are delighted to welcome the how-to-become-famous book. Not successful, you understand, not loved or happy: just famous.

The newest, brashest one is called *HYPE! The Essential Guide to Marketing Yourself* (Hutchinson) and the author, Andrew Crofts, explains in its preface that 'there has never been a better time to become famous'.

Warhol's casual era of fame for fifteen minutes has been replaced by something more professional: a need to 'work hard at your reputation and make sure you are skilled at being famous'. Anyone can do it, Mr Crofts promises: not just actors or writers or television bimbettes, but business people, lawyers, academics – anyone who might like the idea of turning up on the Nine O'Clock News labelled 'expert', having his home life written up by Sunday magazines, and being rung up at all hours by harassed journalists demanding quotes on the state of the industry.

Mr Crofts has his shining examples, some of whom may be positively insulted to be included. He reveres the images of Richard

118

Branson, Peter de Savary, Frederick Forsyth and Bob Geldof. Mr Geldof comes in for particular approval because he not only became a world figure through Live Aid, but managed to use the associated fame to get razor-blades and milk commercials. 'An anonymous charity worker in a safari jacket and horn-rimmed spectacles, who had worked for years in the back office at Oxfam,' says Mr Crofts scornfully, 'could have done neither.'

The golden road away from horn-rimmed obscurity depends only on your determination. 'Every industry provides opportunity for self-promotion at some stage,' promises the author, sketching a fanciful scenario in which 'an accountant with a company which makes filing cabinets' manages to whip up a storm of controversy about the future of the paperless office, gets in to the local papers, then the nationals . . . and, by imputation, ends up hosting his own television show with Anneka Rice.

Television professionals will flinch at the man's advice to bombard producers with drinks, letters and closely-written synopses of tele-vision shows 'as long as you will be the central character in the series . . . don't forget that our primary objective is to make you famous, not to make you a television writer.' Editors will also be cowed and repelled by the fearful singlemindedness of this fame-crazed filing cabinet salesman, who strafes them with unsolicited columns and 'makes it clear that he doesn't expect to be paid'. Vanity publishing gets the nod, a book gives 'credibility', even if nobody reads it.

Like any marketing man, you must constantly update the product – yourself – and 'imbue it with new unique selling points'. So if you give to charity, do it noisily: if you marry, 'do it in the full glare of the spotlight', like Derek Jameson.

Mr Crofts cannot be blamed: he speaks for the times, and there will be more *HYPE!* books, plenty of them. His methods might even work (though if they do, how come I have never heard of him?). But what is chilling is that financial rewards seem hardly to matter to his self-salesmen. They just want to be famous. They give up privacy, dignity, modesty and a sense of humour for a flickering, phantom half-life on the screens of strangers. And even if it works, they know they will end up hiding. 'Sometimes,' says Mr Crofts with the air of a man who knows, 'it is impossible to live up to one's own reputation for greatness.'

How true, how very true.

35

Can't we all learn to love a boilermaker?

*R*ight at the end of the protesting 1960s, when every wall bore a thrilling left-wing slogan, I had a haughty blue-blooded flat-mate. One day she sighed contentedly, stretched her chic, denim-clad legs and said in her cut-glass tones: 'You know, Purves, it's apslootly marvellous. I was brought up to despise people who were in Trade. That's way out of date, of course, but the great thing now is that I can call it capitalism and despise it just the same.'

She had learned the secret of her generation: how to slide effort-lessly from old-fashioned Establishment snootiness to new-fangled Leftish idealism without even bumping on the join. From consider-ing commerce to be full of vulgar oiks, she moved without difficulty into regarding it as the preserve of wicked capitalists in top hats, watering the workers' beer.

I thought of her last week when Peter Morgan, the new director-general of the Institute of Directors, launched his attack on the Establishment for not supporting industry.

He castigated the Church, middle classes and intelligentsia for their 'pernicious views'. Instead of applauding the wonderful wealth-creators in our midst, he says, they ungratefully condemn the 1980s as a decade of greed and materialism. For them, only the distribution of wealth is a noble activity: 'Creating it is mucky and squalid.'

Poor Mr Morgan: every profit he creates is ruined for him by the awful suspicion that Harold Pinter, Lady Antonia Fraser and the Bishop of Liverpool are sneering at him and that thousands of people in stripped-pine kitchens are making disparaging remarks about his salary.

I recognize the symptoms well. Such is our national haughtiness about commerce that British industrialists are still paranoid about this even after years of sabre-toothed Thatcherism.

For instance, whenever I, an ignorant media type, go to lunch with them in the hope of hearing all about industry, they just say modest, defensive things like: 'Oh, we're just a bunch of valve manufacturers. Very boring. Tell me, what's Terry Wogan really like?' If a young man goes into his family's thriving compressed-air business, he knows in his heart that he is cutting himself off forever from being cited in *The Face* as a style setter and that he is unlikely ever to be invited to do Thought for the Day from the perspective of the plant-hire industry. The only branches of commerce to attain a sort of stylish acceptability recently have been those which border on showbiz, advertising, public relations and shrieking down telephones in merchant banks. Occasionally a self-made millionaire like Richard Branson or Alan Sugar becomes a sort of media star, whereupon everyone exclaims what fun he is – in an amazed tone of voice, as if for a self-made businessman to show any human qualities at all was a miracle akin to a talking dog. No wonder Mr Morgan is disgruntled. Profit is not enough: a man needs praise too.

Perhaps we need a new school of novels to express the great romance of commerce. They used to in the last century: ah, how I used to thrill to John Halifax, Gentleman, bravely building up the tannery by his own efforts!

We must make sure that in the next Andrea Newman drama she doesn't fob us off with another bunch of writers and painters and probation officers, but sets her torrid passions in a thriving export glassworks. We must urge Salman Rushdie to spend his exile in writing a best-selling history of Blue Circle Cement plc. We must learn to thrill to industry.

Meanwhile, to cheer him up, Mr Morgan might like to reflect on what happens to those our perverse society actually does respect: nurses, ambulancemen, firemen, mothers . . .

They are all, unfortunately, broke.

36

After-dinner artistry

The after-dinner speaker, rising to face his tipsy audience, may be disconcerted to realize that he is being judged not only by them but also – and dispassionately – by the grand figure in brass buttons who has just prayed silence for him. But it must be so: every year the Guild of Professional Toastmasters solemnly confers before presenting its award to its After-Dinner Speaker of the Year. Its interpretation of after-dinner speaking is rather loose: this year [1989] Margaret Thatcher has won the elegant rosewood gavel for her Tory conference speech. The only other Prime Minister to be so honoured was Harold Wilson.

But wherever seasoned speakers meet to compare their wounds, there will be some resentful mutterings. After all, Mrs Thatcher had an Autocue machine, a carefully designed stage-set and a loyal, hand-picked audience. Would she have been as effective faced with a dog-eared pack of index cards, a howling microphone and a roomful of sozzled Rotarians?

Even the ritziest of £1,000-a-night speakers has to contend with some or all of these handicaps. Those of us who operate rather lower down the financial scale suffer even worse indignities. I have never forgotten the chairperson who cheerily said: 'Thank you. Old Mrs Wetherby stayed awake nearly to the end, which is always a good sign,' especially as I had been muffing every punch-line in the last ten minutes because of my growing conviction that Mrs Wetherby had died in her chair. And John Timpson, an old warhorse of the after-dinner circuit, once reported the harrowing experience of getting his fee paid at the table, counted out in florins from the raffle-money tin.

The art of after-dinner speaking involves more than just owning a good speech. Such smoothies as Cecil Parkinson and Jeffrey Archer give chillingly polished performances, but they don't raise the roof. A certain vulnerability and sense of danger is necessary for real rapport. Relaxed audiences like a speaker who sounds as if he (or she) is making it up on the hoof, and might get indiscreet at any moment. This is a magical feeling, generated by the most unexpected people: the Princess Royal, at private, unreported dinners, is surprisingly spontaneous and very funny.

Part of the knack is sizing up the audience, its interests, intelligence, sobriety and moral tone. Mrs Thatcher is used to addressing the Tory Party, so in fairness she should have had a handicap. In the front line of real after-dinner speakers you are faced with an unquantifiable company: one showbiz acquaintance was in the act of rising to his feet at a business dinner when the chairman leant across and hissed 'Nothing mucky!' He slammed in a mental filter just in time to turn the VD joke into one about a parrot.

If Mrs Thatcher's well-supported polish earns her the rosewood gavel, there should be some lesser prizes, too – a cheap pine version, maybe, awarded to a real trouper for courage in adversity. I would favour the literary-luncheon hack who bravely struggles from city to city with his pile of books, preaching to hatted ladies and bored booksellers full of duchesse potatoes.

I once – only once – spoke at two literary lunches in the same week, and my fellow-speaker at both was Gerald Durrell. Meeting on the second day we looked at one another in mild dismay. Durrell said, 'Tell you what. You do my speech, I'll do yours. I can remember most of it.' If we had dared, we should both have got gavels for it. Compressed-sawdust ones, perhaps.

37

Duel careers

*W*oodman, spare that mistletoe! For the duration, at least, of the office party season. Here is a warning to those who – in defiance of probability and cruel industrial strip-lighting – find their colleagues attractive. Don't do it. Fight the impulse. It gets you sacked.

The warning came from the Labour Research organization, which has uncovered continuing hostility to office romance on the part of many managements. This is grim news for those unattached people who only ever meet anybody at the office, but there it is. Labour Research found examples of people sacked for falling in love too visibly, who subsequently got no sympathy from industrial tribunals. Honourable intentions make it even worse: many employers still hold rigidly to the ancient rule that wives and husbands may not work together in the same department. Office marriages are still prone to result in sackings and demotings, again upheld by tribunals.

I was surprised to find that the old prejudice still has so much life in it. I thought the last two decades would have eroded it away. What about all this caring, sharing new-age management of which we hear so much? What about those office-ensemble TV series like Capital City, where Declan weds Michelle and all the Eurobond traders hug each other significantly at the wedding before racing back to corner the peseta? And in real life, we are forever invited to marvel at such pigeon pairs as Peter and Virginia Bottomley, the Branaghs, and Sir Nicholas and Lady Lloyd editing the Daily and Sunday Expresses *con amore*. Look at our popular culture: Richard Madeley and Judy Finnegan simper side by side on the Granada sofa, and Anne Diamond occupies the BBC one with a stage 'husband', Nick Owen – and her real one Mike Hollingsworth as producer. Open any magazine and there is a Laura-and-Bernard Ashley retrospective, or a pair of lovebirds writing sitcoms on his 'n' hers word processors. Husbands and wives working together, an informed Martian would conclude, are the coming thing.

I have no personal axe to grind here: rather the reverse. Some of us (never mind why) have actually been evading it by the skin of our teeth for years. My own dear husband and I have twice narrowly escaped from co-presenting programmes: a prospect which horrified him so much that he turned to a new career planting mangel-wurzels and hauling lambs out of sheep's back ends at 3 am, reasoning correctly that this greatly reduces the risk of my turning up as his little helpmeet.

But plenty of others manage fine. Calm and rational couples confine themselves to business talk in the office and only sometimes, alone together in the lift, allow intimacy to break through in the form of curt mutual instructions about PTAs and Sanilav. I knew one pair so formal that temps used to take weeks to realize they were married at all. The prissiness of moving couples apart, like a schoolteacher separating best friends in class, seems a curiously dated manoeuvre. Even if a marriage does happen to be stormy enough to impinge upon work, it would do that anyway. I would have thought it a great saving of the line manager's time if he or she could see the eruption coming.

Which brings us to the really counterproductive hazard of the dual-career family, the one nobody mentions. It isn't husbands and wives working as colleagues that breeds trouble: it is the separate, competitive seesaw of two independent careers. Gossip from the US suggested that Tatum O'Neal and John McEnroe have trouble because *he* didn't like *her* working while the children were small, and now they are bigger *she* wants to be a star again, only *his* tennis career has faltered and he would feel small if she did.

Whatever the truth of that, the principle is horribly familiar. There is nothing harder than to accept a promotion or celebrate a coup when your partner is on a downward slope. Unless it is to crack open the champagne for a wife's or husband's advancement, while tactfully holding back for a few days the news of precisely what happened to you in the Outplacement Consultant's office this morning. A spouse's big break should be – often is – cause for selfless celebration and joint planning of a big spend; but oh, it can be gall and wormwood and a bitter, thwarted twisting in the gut.

But nobody thinks about that, do they? They say tactless things about you 'not needing to work so hard now' that your spouse is flying high, and how it must be a blessing in disguise that Denise got the European job you went for. And even the most loving, nicest men and women grind their teeth and suffer in silence. While their managers, it appears, are still back in 1955, busy fussing about office romances.

38

Spiderwoman

Superwoman! What can have possessed the National Council of Women to put that moth-eaten, discredited, tatty old bird in the title of their report on women and work?

Its full name was 'Superwoman keeps going – Understanding the female web'. The web image was better, suggesting fewer heroics and more complexity: perhaps we should switch to Spiderwoman as a role-model. This would have the added advantage of acknowledging the muted horror with which many men (and Barbara Cartland, of course) still view career-minded women. Female spiders, remember, not only weave webs: they eat males alive. For all we know, they probably accuse them of sexual harassment too, and refuse to make coffee, and wear really annoying clickety stiletto heels round the office. Yes, Spiderwoman it is.

The NCW report got varied coverage. The *Standard* had a quick look and decided on the headline 'Superwoman finds staying home is best'. The *Independent* and *Guardian* came up with the opposite reading – the former saying 'Women put priority on working life'. The *Telegraph* settled for 'The Superwoman Trap' and noted that children have 'slipped to third place as a priority', while the *Mirror* was even more shocked, with 'Mum's Not the Word' and the revelation that 87 per cent of females aged 16–44 say a woman does not need a child in order to feel fulfilled, and 'voted a husband and kids a poor third' to hobbies and work. The words 'selfish cows!' were not actually printed, but they sort of hovered, unspoken.

I read the full report, being curious about this 'third place' apparently held by Spiderwoman's family life. It turned out that the question was not about how you actually spend your time, but what you 'would like to spend more time on'. It was, in other words, a measure of wishful thinking. So, naturally, the great majority spoke of hobbies and education. Only 15 per cent wanted extra time with their families – but considering that they had already explained that their family currently took up most of their energy, this seems not unreasonable. What do they want, blood?

As for the much-flagged 'Children are not fulfilling' line, it is true that 87 per cent of the under-44s refused to agree that 'a woman needs a child to be fulfilled'. But so what? Women without children are bound to deny it, some from happy experience and others because they are reluctant to burst into tears during a telephone opinion poll. Meanwhile, even the most doting mothers have learned over the years not to patronize their childless sisters as much as they did in the fifties ('Poor Auntie Vera'). Apart from anything else, the said sisters are too useful as babysitters and whizzy bachelor aunties to risk annoying them. For heaven's sake, surely it is a cause for robust rejoicing that only 13 per cent of us are so tediously mumsy as to consider a childless woman disabled?

But the most interesting, and least headlined, aspect of the report was on women's confidence at work. The juggling of childcare and social duties seems, on my reading, to be registering a modest improvement. Where pain showed through the figures it was not about time-management. It was about the yearning to have your skills recognized and used. A lot of these bustling, competent, juggling women are, it seems to me, quite sad. Or they risk becoming so, the moment their families ease off the pressure.

Look at the figures: three-quarters feel they are only half educated. The same proportion want to get on further in their work, yet less than half have dared to plan how. And a large number are resigned to the fact that they won't, ever. A third speak longingly of unused skills: they are 'organizing and communicating' (i.e. being PAs) and want to be 'practical, analytical and problem-solving'.

Yet they hang back, tearful. Even among the youngest women, a quarter are wary of taking on a higher profile at work. A third have slowed down to have children, and know what this will cost them. Only half reckon that senior managers have any interest in their career, and most see their promotion prospects as bad. The NCW observes that family women 'have no time to get off the treadmill' and plan for themselves.

Oh yes, there is sadness here. Not a feminist grudge, but the sadness of unfulfilled individual dreams. I keep thinking of a classic BBC interview with an old lady called Bella Keyser, who glimpsed her personal paradise when she worked in the wartime shipyards. Then the men came back, and she spent the next thirty years trying to work again as a welder. All she wanted, she said, was to see 'that beautiful thing, a ship' forming out of chaos, and her own hands helping it grow. Every word she spoke conjured up a pain that both sexes knew equally: the pain of a missed vocation.

If more managers were attuned to that note of hungry ambition, and recognized it as readily in the 35-year-old mother returning to work as in the bright young lad alongside her, who knows what joyful energies they might not tap? If not, then grieve for Bella: grieve for poor tangled Spiderwoman, stuck in her own endless, circular web of clever arrangements, juggling handfuls of nothing much.

39

Byting the hand

We have just celebrated twenty-five years of the hole-in-the-wall cash machine. Incredible: it seems only yesterday that as a fed-up student tourist guide I used to tell Americans in Oxford that the thing halfway up the High Street was put there in 1492 in pious memory of St Robert de Barclaycash. Some of them even took photographs of it. The quarter-century celebrations appear to have been muted, consisting largely of a carping ten minutes on Radio 4's You and Yours about phantom withdrawals, but I would like to pay a lone tribute.

For those automatic tellers were pioneering educators: they were the very first computer screens which my generation was forced to confront. They were the first to introduce us to the blank uncomprehending fury brought on by encountering something at once brilliant, logical and moronic. But they gave us cash at night when we liked spending it best, and saved us from the risk of meeting the bank manager face-to-face, so we soldiered on: nervously typed in our secret codes, waited for prompts and when the machine winked 'Incorrect code' groped in vain for a button marked 'Look, it's me, honestly, it can't be more than one digit out!' or 'All right, you electronic cleverclogs, how do you suggest I get home?' Bleeping remorselessly, the machines taught us a new and crucial truth: that in the late twentieth century if you cannot relate correctly to a screen, you are on the scrapheap of history.

It was hard to accept. Computers respond as no person, animal or device in the history of the world has ever responded before.

You cannot reason with them, coax them or thump them. They are Vulcan invaders. And very recently landed: computers may now seem commonplace, but I can prove how new this is. In 1972 I was a temp typist in an industrial training office in North London. Here, amid clouds of powdered Tipp-Ex and a powerful reek of Snopake correcting fluid, we rattled out lists of trainees and made six carbon copies of the canteen menus. Around us reared filing cabinets full of quaint mistypings about the Hongkong and Shanghai Banging Corporation and the Lloyds Policy Singing Office. And whose name was over the door? IBM, no less. We were at the heart of the computer industry, processing COBOL trainees daily; yet there was no suggestion of bleep or cursor ever being likely to disturb the placid waters of our placid typing-pool. Computers were for specialists. Big boys. And so they remained, until they became toys for the first generation of obsessives to programme their BBC Micros in the back bedroom. This too lasted until very recently; it is but yesterday that the aliens invaded the rest of us.

So even today, when every snotty rising-five in the primary school classroom can insouciantly bang away on keys with teddy-bear stickers on them; when every ten-thumbed journalist carries a laptop miracle already grimed with age and beer, dread of computers still runs deep. Tabloids thrive on stories about bills for £0.00p and children who have freak fits playing computer screen games. Scaremongers wring their hands over 'computer addiction' (the disease of children whose parents are too wet to say 'switch it off!'). Even in the most high-tech offices and reception desks you can still watch workers in the state which trauma specialists know as 'Denial': watch them peck nervously at a couple of keys, peer at the screen, and jerk back with both hands in the air going 'Aaaaaaah! – ' before fleeing to seek advice. But the computer is probably behaving no worse than the old filing cabinet did when you put the manila folder in crooked, and it caught in the hinge and spilled dockets down the wainscoting.

I claim no smug proficiency. Mrs Bird could testify to this: she being the motherly consultant who came last week to teach me my new grown-up computer. She clearly got my measure when – after an hysterical enquiry as to why I had to bother with 'trees' and 'wildcards' anyway – she said 'Think of your hard disk as a big filing cabinet. You wouldn't just throw documents in all higgledy-piggledy, would you?', and I said yes, actually, I would.

Others who could bear witness against me are the two software experts, engineer and systems manager who have been attempting for five days, as I write, to steer me through the shoals of data-bits and parities, atx3 prompts and RS232s which are supposed to make these words fly down a telephone line at 2400 bauds per whatsit and land in the News International computer (Look, no hands!). I am not good at this. All through the recent fuss about video games giving children fits, my son was downstairs, decorously playing SuperMarioLand while in the study I jerked, foamed at the mouth and sobbed in fury because yet another man had chided me for being in the wrong flow-control mode or not resetting my emulations ('Prestel is a Videotex emulation, see? So you want your pop-up menu . . .')

But at least I want to learn, and not to be afraid and angry and obsolete and middle-aged and Luddite. Before my screen each night I shall light a votive cursor and murmur a prayer to St Robert de Barclaycash, author of the miracle of the midnight fivers a quarter of a century ago.